MIND OF
A SUPERIOR
HITTER:

THE ART, SCIENCE, AND
PHILOSOPHY

MICHAEL MCCREE

MICHAEL MCCREE

Contact Author By: michael.gamechanger@gmail.com
The purpose of the information contained in this book is to educate players in baseball and softball on how to enhance the performance. Nothing contained in this book should be construed nor is intended to be used for medical diagnosis or treatment. It should not be used in place of the advice of your physician or other qualified health care provider.
Should you have any health care related questions, please call or see your physician or other qualified health care provider promptly. Always consult with your physician or other qualified health care provider before embarking on a new treatment, diet, or fitness program.
You should never disregard medical advice or delay seeking it because of something you have read in this book.
This book is also available in e-book format.

McCree, Michael.
        Mind of a Superior Hitter: The Art, Science and Philosophy/ by Michael McCree.

ISBN: 978-0-692-05751-3
    1.   Sports- Psychological
    2.   Sports- Baseball
    3.   Sports- Softball
    4.   Baseball-Coaching
    5.   Softball- Coaching

Book Cover Design by Leslie K. © 2018 Super Massive 3D

Printed in the United States of America

Table of Contents

Other Works by the Author:

The Mental Mastery of Hitting in Baseball, inspired by the book, *Mind of a Superior Hitter: The Art, Science and Philosophy,* delves into the specifics of what it takes to think like a successful hitter. Filled with 2+ hours of interviews from some of the top experts in hitting, this film was designed to encourage players of any age to take ownership of their improvement and performance at the plate.

Available on **Amazon.com** on DVD
and digitally on **Vimeo.com**

Mentalmasteryofbaseball.com

Other Works by the Author:

GameChanger: The Baseball Parent's Ultimate Guide is a unique work created by baseball trainer Michael McCree to communicate the best ways baseball parents can raise and guide their aspiring ball players. This book is designed to help parents realize that they can acquire the knowledge it takes to make a meaningful impact in the ongoing development of their youth baseball player (*applicable to softball as well. Ages 5-13*), regardless of prior understanding of the game.

The information presented in *GameChanger: The Baseball Parent's Ultimate Guide* will transform the way parents think about issues pertaining to youth baseball. The subject matter, written by a former collegiate baseball player with over 20 years of playing and private training experience, includes topics like character building, managing expectations, overcoming slumps, dealing with injuries, and teaching the mental aspect of baseball.

CHAPTER 1

KEY ASPECTS OF A GREAT HITTER

You don't have to be a total genius to be a great hitter. However, there are some very important principles that anyone must follow in order to become a superior hitter in both baseball and softball. Those with the most *effective* approach at the plate have a greater chance of significantly increasing their probability of success. Both their physical and mental components must be in harmony or else their chances of succeeding will be slim. Not all hitters use identical methods to arrive at a successful hitting approach. There are *multiple* ways for players, of all levels, to develop a winning style of hitting, yet there *are* some core elements that should be used to ensure a greater deal of consistency in the batter's box. Knowing what areas to focus on, mentally and physically, is what's most important to anyone that seeks to be an offensive force as a hitter.

Even though the keys to hitting are rather simple in nature, the process of transformation requires more of a scientific method of asking the right questions and seeking to find the right answers that best fit each player as a unique individual.

Statistically, the very best hitters to ever play have had career averages of around .300 or better (a 30% success rate). The margins between a successful hitter and an unsuccessful one can be rather slim. A player getting one extra hit per ten at-bats would be the difference of going three-for-ten versus going four-for-ten. This seemingly small difference per ten at-bats over an entire season would result in one batting average being .300 and the other being .400—a major difference when referring to statistics for an entire season. However, if a hitter sees their progression in this way, it could be less overwhelming. If a player simply strives to improve enough to at least manage just one extra hit per ten at-bats, it could make a major difference in the long run.

Let's discuss the four major areas that all hitters undoubtedly need to focus their attention on.

THE FOUR KEY ASPECTS OF A GREAT HITTER

Mindset

At the higher levels of the game, the pitcher-hitter matchups become more like a chess game. As pitchers gain more control of their pitches and as hitters get more bat control, bat speed, and skill, it takes more than just raw talent and natural-born athleticism. Stepping up to the plate without a winner's mindset will cause a batter to be too reactionary and will stifle the focus and *intent* of the hitter—the clear and unwavering intent of stepping into the box with an idea of what the outcome will be from the at-bat. Mindset deals with your will to compete at a high level. The proper mindset may be the most readily available trait to acquire because it doesn't take talent, only sheer will and determination, which can be obtained instantly after a player *decides* they *want* to change for the better.

Philosophy

What is your "mission statement" as a hitter? The mindset is more from an attitude perspective while philosophy deals more with strategy and a focused game plan. Mindset can get you hyped up and ready to go while the philosophy gives you the blueprint on how to execute the plan. A hitter with a strong hitting philosophy won't simply *guess* the next pitch or *hope* that something good will happen. Do you know what you want to accomplish in this at-bat or are you simply going to wing it and just see how things turn out?

Technique

This involves hitting the correct way, which will create more consistent results. A hitter can know the philosophy and have the mindset, but without technique, it will be harder to get the results they need on a *consistent* basis. It pertains to the things that a batter needs to do *physically*, such as using the correct form, balance, and swing path. This will also include things like

- Stance
- Point of contact
- Follow through
- Finish

Timing

Without timing, technique doesn't have the opportunity to play its role in the swing. Aside from having the right mindset and philosophy as a hitter, this is the most important. Even a hitter with flattering technique or gifted with physical strength will not be able to hit consistently without the *timing*. You simply can't hit the ball if your bat isn't in the hitting zone at the time that the ball is crossing the plate. Even those who have bad technique have a chance at a decent hit as long as they have the right timing.

If one of these four areas are lacking, you need even more from the other three to compensate.

For example, a lack in mindset will cause for a player to need an even better hitting philosophy in order to stay afloat, but that's just one instance. Here are a few more examples of potential combinations where a lack of one can be balanced by the help of the others.

Good Mindset/Good Technique/Good Timing/**Bad Philosophy**

Good Mindset/Good Philosophy/Good Timing/**Bad Technique**

Good Mindset/Good Philosophy/Good Technique/**Bad Timing**

Good Philosophy/Good Technique/Good Timing/**Bad Mindset**

Good Philosophy/Good Mindset/Good Timing/**Bad Technique**

Good Philosophy/Good Mindset/Good Technique/**Bad Timing**

Good Technique/Good Philosophy/Good Timing/**Bad Mindset**

Good Technique/Good Timing/Good Mindset/**Bad Philosophy**

Good Technique/Good Mindset/Good Philosophy/**Bad Timing**

Good Timing/Good Philosophy/Good Technique/**Bad Mindset**

Good Timing/Good Technique/Good Mindset/**Bad Philosophy**

Good Timing/Good Mindset/Good Philosophy/**Bad Technique**

Take a good look at each combination and see where you fit in as a hitter. You can have at least three of these areas intact and still be able to have a decent chance at becoming a consistent hitter. Of course, you always have an even better chance as a hitter if you can become efficient at all four areas. Some hitters are fortunate enough to be able to get away with only having two of these qualities. These hitters are obviously even more at the mercy of good pitchers whenever they face them, but it doesn't mean they don't stand a chance at all.

- Physically speaking, the two most important areas mentioned above are *technique* and *timing*.

- Mentally speaking, the two most important areas mentioned above are *mindset* and *philosophy*.

All four (technique, timing, mindset, and philosophy) are interwoven, interdependent, and have an effect on one another.

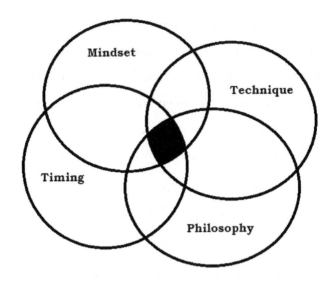

The blacked-out area that the arrow is pointing to in this Venn diagram illustrates where every player should strive to be as a complete hitter. If a player can improve his or her skill level in all four areas, they have the best chance at having a higher batting average. Notice that all areas overlap and have a bearing on one another. Also, notice there are some areas where you could encompass all but one aspect of hitting (like the combinations mentioned earlier). These four areas of hitting can be improved upon regardless of natural ability.

Strength & Power (The Honorable Mention)

Players have to keep in mind that the objective is to get the best out of what they have while understanding that everyone isn't a "power hitter." This fifth variable, unlike the other four, has a ceiling for most players. Smaller players can only get so much stronger. Strength is linked to physical capability and not so much on how often you work on cultivating it. Even though you can spend a lot of time attempting to increase strength, those who are not physically capable of being consistent homerun hitters can only do so much to max out their power. This is why it is important to work within the parameters of a hitter's maximum capacity.

All four of the unchangeable core principles of a complete hitter plus the fifth variable of power create the most well-rounded player. The five elements are like all five fingers on a hand, each working independently of one another yet more capable as a unit—able to lift one finger at a time yet able to throw a powerful punch when used together.

Be proud of the areas you are strong in, while still paying attention to what needs improvement. Some hitters may be above average in one or more of the areas above yet may also struggle in one or more area. The objective is to maintain the skills you already have in your current strengths while constantly upgrading the areas where you need enhancement.

There are two types of hitters—the one you are and the one you know you *can* be. What stands in the way of your transition from the hitter you are *now* to the one you want to *become* isn't always a physical matter (i.e. strength or technique). It usually lies in the knowledge that is acquired and then applied—what a hitter learns and, more importantly, what they *implement*.

"TO BE A GOOD
HITTER YOU'VE GOT
TO DO ONE THING –
GET A GOOD BALL TO
HIT."

ROGERS HORNSBY

CHAPTER 2

QUALITY vs. QUANTITY

How you hit during practice is more important than *how many*.

The quality of the practice habits that a hitter has are the keys to building a solid and consistent swing. Many people believe that good old-fashioned hard work is all that's needed for becoming a supreme hitter. When it comes down to it, hard work can actually harm a player's swing if they aren't doing it *correctly*. If their swing is not being done correctly, they will end up practicing bad habits over and over, which will solidify a defective technique. This is why making sure that in practice, *quality* always comes before *quantity*. Only when a hitter reaches a level of *quality* in their swing through training with the right coach, asking the right questions, or studying the right amount of video will quantity best serve them. It isn't until those things are done that their quantity of repetitions will be of benefit. Practicing the wrong way repetitively will only help you get better at doing the *wrong* things.

A hitter deciding to just "swing until they figure it out" could very well be leading themselves down a path of destruction. Although, *some* players can recover from years of bad habits, it's not recommended to go that route if you don't have to. The less time you spend practicing a bad technique as a hitter, the less amount of time you will spend teaching your body the wrong technique through muscle memory.

It must be a player's utmost priority to make sure that quality is always at the forefront of their intention upon the start of each practice session. This means that ten minutes of quality practice time is more effective than an hour of lackadaisical practice. Ten swings done properly is more effective than one hundred swings done without focus and attention.

The biggest obstacle to maintaining quality when practicing is **concentration.** Aside from being given the necessary knowledge of the most effective way to swing, *concentration* is one of the most important foundations of a quality training or practice session. It's the main thing that separates quality from quantity. Without the right amount of *concentration*, a hitter's mind can wander into their own dream world. The focus is much easier to keep when practice has just begun, but once a hitter has taken a certain amount of swings, they are more likely to lose focus on what matters.

Daydreaming about what's for dinner or the fun you and your friends are going to have at the movies over the weekend will start to creep in. When you take your mind away from making sure that you are practicing correctly, your body can start to revert back to bad habits without you even being aware of it. Even though your mind is not fully engaged in the swing, your body always is.

Remember that our bodies memorize movements, the good and the bad. This is why we must keep a close guard on every movement we make while practicing. It is best to do this until we've developed the ideal swing pattern and can rely more on our proper muscle memory from many hours and swings. Until the muscle memory sets in, a very special attention has to be given to each and every movement that takes place. Attention to detail must be at an all-time high.

WHAT IS A "QUALITY DRILL"?

Is there such a thing as a bad drill for a hitter to practice? Often coaches or just people in general within the baseball and softball communities, will discuss what constitutes a good drill or a bad drill. Truthfully, *any* drill you partake in can be a "bad drill" if it isn't being done right. Some may perceive a drill as being bad simply because they don't understand or see the value in what is being taught or teaching it correctly.

For example, an onlooker may complain about a drill simply because they are not fully knowledgeable to what the drill teaches. Quality training has to start with quality instruction and learning. A good teacher and good student go hand-in-hand. A player willing to learn and grow as a hitter with no one there to teach them will result in not reaching their potential at the rate in which they are possible, which doesn't mean they *can't*.

The same thing goes for an instructor or coach willing *and* capable to teach the information necessary to a hitter trying to improve their game, but if the player isn't willing to be a good listener in order to incorporate the instruction into their game, it won't have a good result.

Getting Creative

Softball great, Laura Berg, recalled a time in college when she had to get creative with her training regimen.

> *"In college, I would take my mattress off of my bed and put it up against the wall in my room and hit balls off of a construction cone (used in place of a tee). I was able to get tons of repetitions this way."*

This may sound obsessive to some, but to those who want to be great, nothing will stop them from expanding their creativity in order to get the job done.

WHY IT'S IMPORTANT TO SLOW IT DOWN

Doing drills at full speed can sometimes make it difficult to tell whether or not a drill is being done correctly. Usually, the hitter can't see what they are doing throughout the swing without the help of video or a mirror. They also may not be in tune with their swing enough to be able to *feel* if something is going wrong with their technique or form.

Performing the swing slowly will help to make sure that hitters do not miss any steps with their swings. Dry swings are great for all hitters. A dry swing would be equal to a boxer doing what's called shadowboxing during training. So, the hitter isn't actually hitting a ball during a dry swing. Instead, they are essentially envisioning themselves hitting an imaginary ball. The slower you perform a dry swing, the easier it is to be able to catch when you are doing something wrong like rolling over with the top hand, dipping the back shoulder, dropping the hands, etc.

A hitter should always seek to swing at less than full speed when concentrating on developing technique, especially while correcting a specific defect in the swing. Slow motion drills help heighten the attention to detail.

Using a full length mirror is also a great tool in helping hitters while doing slow-motion drills. Since video analysis is not always available for all players, mirrors can serve as a means of giving a hitter an opportunity to see what they're doing. It's much easier to catch mistakes in technique when swings are done slowly and with attention to detail.

It also allows the mind and the body an opportunity to get on the same page, as the body has a mind of its own through muscle memory. The dynamics of muscle memory are complex, but in order to undo it or reprogram the body, a hitter must use a high level of concentration. This part of the transformation takes *patience*.

The *discipline* required for the patience that is necessary to unlearn bad habits is crucial. Without it, a hitter will try to rush through the reprogramming phrase of their technique and skip over important steps. Attempting to change technique at full speed will make it very hard to ensure the hitter is doing it correctly. Slowing things down helps players with paying attention to detail and helps for them to not miss a step in the process of the swing.

Players that normally swing as hard as physically possible usually have difficulty with this. It's a *habit* for them to attempt to hit the ball as hard as they can, which could make it difficult to fix flaws in their technique. If hitters aren't careful, they could end up giving in mentally due to the lack of results. The frustration of not having enough discipline and patience can weigh heavily as a factor in success.

It's fairly easy to take things slow when you are by yourself and doing training alone off of a hitting tee or doing dry swings. However, when you are with a partner or at team practice, you will encounter others who will not take their time with their swing repetitions in the same way that you wish to. You may be partnered with someone during soft toss who is moving too quickly for you to focus on each repetition.

In situations like this, you can ask your partner to slow things down a little bit, respectfully explaining to them that you have something to work on. It only takes a second to say something like

"Hey, I'm working on my timing. Could you slow it down a tad so that I can work on getting my hands ready before the pitch?"

Good teammates usually don't have a problem with a request like this. In fact, if you are partnering with the *right* teammate, they will want to make sure that *they* too will pay attention to the small details.

PICKING A GOOD TEAMMATE TO WORK WITH

When in the solitude of your own training session at home or in a secluded environment, it is easier to have fewer external distractions and for your plans to have a solid, concentrated and productive hitting session be a success. However, what do you do when you are in a team setting? It is much harder to control team settings to fit your own personal agenda.

A hitter making sure that they buddy-up with a teammate who will be willing to help them *focus* is most important. Having a best friend on the team that you like to laugh and joke with is fun. Being in a team setting and having a brotherhood or sisterhood is one of the most exciting things about being on a team. This is why it's harder to stay completely focused at all times while in a team setting—jokes and funny stories are being told and everyone is cracking smiles and enjoying themselves.

Therefore, it is so important to choose wisely when you decide who to work with during drills.

WHEN YOU GET FRUSTRATED

From time to time, a hitter will struggle when working on their swing in their private time or even at team practice. This is a time where they must dig deep and find their mental strength and discipline. There is something that takes place when a hitter is having an off day with their swing that can makes them very *angry*.

But this is also a time to see what they are truly made of. Their body language starts to show disappointment, and they start to let out loud sighs and moans to show their frustration. It creates anxiety for hitters who want so badly to do well but just can't seem to find their groove on a particular day. This is completely understandable, especially when a hitter *knows* they are capable of doing much better. However, they must keep in mind that not all days at the ballpark will be good days. Not every swing is going to be to perfection.

This is why most people will say that baseball and softball are 90% mental and 10% physical. The physical part will come after the mental side is improved. A hitter must *always* keep their focus on maintaining the mental aspect of themselves. Enhancing your focus takes work and during practice is a perfect time to improve this.

If you take more than two swings that you feel may be off, regroup by doing the following.

1. Step away from the batter's box.

2. Take a few deep breaths to clear your mind.

3. Grab a drink of water if you need to.

4. Keep a positive outlook.

5. Identify what you need to do better.

6. Take a couple of dry swings.

7. Get back into the box focused and ready to work.

Never judge yourself when you aren't doing well. Never say, "I suck!" or things like, "I'll never get this right." Always have the mentality that you can and *will* do better. Take it one swing at a time. Make your hitting sessions more of a *thinking* exercise while physically working on your skills. Use it as a time for your mind and body to become one and connect. Train your body to submit to the commands of your mind.

This is the time to figure out how to do these things. During a game certainly isn't the time for discovering these connections with yourself. During the game, all that should be thought about is getting a good pitch to hit. It isn't the time to think about technique, which is why it is important to work these things out in controlled settings like practices.

Anger also will *not* help. It will only cloud the mind of a hitter and make them do things they do not want to do like swing at bad pitches. To be able to train with *quality* as the focal point, there needs to be a sense of peace and tranquility in the hitter's mind. Anger and frustration can be enough to make you *want* to work harder to get better, but *sustained* anger will be detrimental to the cause. You should calmly *think* your way through these tough times. Some batters get really mad and feel that swinging harder will help them to get back on the right track.

Self-control is a major characteristic that needs to be developed by all hitters who desire to dominate their opponents. Self-control represents maturity, which is perhaps the most important characteristic for smart hitters.

Resilience is key to endure drills that are mentally and physically difficult. The better a player gets at certain drills, the more fun they become. A player who claims to hate a particular drill is someone who is having a hard time mastering that drill because they may need improvement. Superior-minded hitters don't run from the challenge of doing a drill that is difficult. Putting your ego to the side and doing what needs to be done to take your game to the next level is of most importance.

THE TEE

When talking about quality training for hitters, you cannot discuss the topic without bringing up one of the most essential tools in training, the batting tee.

A batting tee offers a wide range of training benefits including hand-eye coordination for younger hitters, bat path and barrel manipulation for seasoned hitters, and overall skill building for players of all ages and skill levels.

Some players use a tee for warming up before a game while others practice more advanced hitting mechanics while doing specific routines. Tee work can be done alone or with a coach. Normally, the balls are hit into a net or fence, so the hitter does not have to spend time picking up an outfield full of balls. Another plus for parents and coaches is the convenience.

Tee workstations can be set up just about anywhere. This allows every hitter on the team to get multiple repetitions during practices. While batting practice with live pitching is great, not every coach can throw a great deal of pitches to every player during practices. Oftentimes, training space is limited, so the tee work station has the ability for players to get work in without having to take up too much area.

A common misconception with those outside of the baseball and softball communities is that a ball player does not need to use a tee as often after they outgrow t-ball, which couldn't be further from the truth. The world's greatest hitters from the past and present have been known to hit off of batting tees, and they do it quite often.

Those who question the necessity of tee work are usually those who are unaware of what it takes to transform a swing and how important it is to a hitter. Building a strong foundation for a swing begins with a batting tee. For starters, adjustments are much more manageable when done using a tee. It provides a hitter the time to figure the swing out in a way that seeing live pitching does not allow because the tee can be moved in or out and up or down to mimic pitches at any height or position in the strike zone and, most of all, can be used for repetitive training to master any given pitch location.

Younger hitters especially have been known to be disinterested in tee work because they don't see it as the cool thing to do. It could appear as boring if the hitter isn't taught the proper usage of the tee and if no one has communicated to them the value to their development. Having a better understanding of *why* the tee is of importance will increase the likelihood of a hitter being much more engaged in the development process when they use it. The more mature and evolved a hitter becomes, the more and more they will rely on tee drills for their transformation.

Former Major League Baseball player Jacob Cruz, who spent almost a decade at the big-league level and who is a current coach in the professional ranks, sees tee drills as a necessary tool for any players that aspire to improve.

"The tee is where you fine tune the swing. This is where you hone your skills and perfect the art of hitting. It takes practice to be a great hitter. It takes discipline to go over the movements again and again and again…and to then do it again the next day. There are no shortcuts. If you don't like the tee, ask yourself 'Why?' If you think that it's boring, then this is not the sport for you."

Cruz designed a hitting device for baseball and softball players called the *LineDrivePro Trainer* available at baseballhittingaid.com

Figure 1. Example of one of the more commonly used generic batting tees of the past decades

The tee in Figure 1 is a picture of one of the most traditionally used tee types. It consists of a fairly hard rubber from top to bottom. Many different manufactures and companies have created their own brand of the same type of tee shown. Over time, these kinds of tees have started to be phased out as technology has improved in innovation and creativity. The downside to a tee of this sort is the hardened rubber and its inability for the hitter to get a true swing on the ball without feeling the thump of the tee stem.

Figure 2. Tanner Tee the Original: Adjustable 26-43 inch

Other types of batting tees are lighter in weight, made of metal, and feature a flexible top that allows hitters to hit through the baseball or softball without feeling any part of the tee. This is very important to training at every level. For young hitters, anticipating bat sting or a sudden thud at contact because of a rigid tee top could cause bad habits. For professional players, they feel that it's important for them to hit the ball and feel only the sweet spot on the ball connecting with the sweet spot of the bat. Shown above is the Tanner Tee. Tanner Tee is one of the top tees in the batting tee industry. Its metal construction, easy adjustments and durable rubber "FlexTop" create a hitting experience that is forgiving for the newest hitters yet very professional for the best.

C.J. Stewart, professional hitting coach and private instructor to several Major League players, is a strong believer in building key habits using the batting tee.

"I coach that there are seven parts to the swing and at least five of them can be developed using the tee. The tee isn't necessarily the best way to help a hitter develop timing or tracking. Only a coach throwing batting practice or doing front toss allows hitters to incorporate all seven parts (those who are kinesthetic learners). Using a tee can be compared to learning to ride a bike with training wheels. If you can learn to ride without training wheels, go for it. The ultimate goal for hitters is getting lots of hits and using a tee is a viable tool for some."

Coach Stewart's 7 Parts to the Swing

1. *Stance/Load*
2. Timing
3. *Tempo*
4. Tracking
5. *Approach*
6. *Contact*
7. *Extension/Finish*

*The five parts of the swing that can be honed while using a tee are in bold-italic.

CHAPTER 3

COMPREHENSION VS. APPLICATION
(Understanding It vs. Doing It)

Understanding what you are supposed to do is not the same as applying what you understand. After being a private hitting trainer for many years, I've seen some clients who have tried over and over again to implement something that they've been taught plenty of times and yet *still* struggle. There is a thin line between knowing *how* to do a thing versus actually *doing* a thing. Take a look at some of the most well-known coaches in college or professional sports.

Very little is known about the playing days of particular championship caliber coaches. They may not have been superstar athletes in their playing days, but they understand enough to be able to teach others how to play the sport the correct way. This is a good example that reminds us that comprehension of something does not equate to being able to apply it.

When it comes to hitting, it's very important to know how to bridge the gap between *knowing* and *doing*. It's great that you *know* the pitcher will throw you a pitch on the outside corner and that you need to keep your weight back and drive the ball to the opposite side of the field, but do you know *how*?

It's great to *know* what technique is required for you to get the most out of your swing. You may be able to recite it in your sleep, but that doesn't constitute being able to *execute*. Execution is key. The best players around the world get paid well for being able to *execute* when the time comes. Coaches and managers at the high levels get paid to *know*, but players get paid to know and, most importantly, *execute*.

WAYS THAT HITTERS CAN LEARN TO APPLY WHAT THEY HAVE LEARNED

Learning to comprehend more about your swing or overall hitting in general requires no abnormal style or method than you would use to gain knowledge in any other field of expertise. Of course, with anything a person aims to improve, the more intensely they study it, and the more they will have a chance of comprehending that subject in a deeper capacity. Since most swings are unique to an individual, it's best to find out about *your* swing as a hitter.

After intense study has been done to find faults in a hitter's swing, they should then work more efficiently and smarter to minimize wasted time to improve more quickly and cut down the learning curve. Working smarter requires getting the most out of *all* training sessions that follow the study time. A good private instructor or trainer can help a hitter with closing this gap.

PRIVATE INSTRUCTORS

It's my belief that all serious hitters should have a designated private hitting instructor to help them on their journey to becoming the hitter they desire to be. Having an extra eye on your swing and someone who can spot the little things that you cannot see is a *huge* benefit. With the right hitting coach, you'll develop the confidence to be able to get back on track when you happen to have setbacks.

A good instructor will have the need to understand the flaws and style of learning of each individual hitter that they work with. A player may be an auditory, visual or kinesthetic learner:

- <u>Auditory Learner</u>: a hitter who learns best through *listening*. They can be corrected and critiqued by hearing certain commands from coaches, and it will be enough for them to understand and make adjustments accordingly.

- <u>Visual Learner</u>: a hitter who learns best through *watching* someone demonstrate a technique. *Hearing* what needs to be changed may not be enough. They may need to *see* video or have someone demonstrate a concept in front of them for them to fully grasp the idea being taught.

- <u>Kinesthetic Learner</u>: a hitter who learns best through using physical movement as a means of sharpening the proper skills in form and technique. (Example: an instructor who takes the bat of a player and moves it in certain directions while the batter is still holding onto the bat in order to get the hitter to *feel* what the instructor is trying to get them to feel.)

Some hitters are better off being exposed to all styles. An instructor's methods do not have to be confined to just one way of teaching. A player may respond to each style to a different extent. For example, a player's learning preference or capacity could have one of the two following breakdowns.

Player #1   Auditory -25%

Visual- 25%

Kinesthetic- 50%

Player #2   Auditory- 30%

Visual- 60%

Kinesthetic- 10%

No two hitters are exactly alike. Not all instructors will resonate with all players. You could be fortunate enough to find a great instructor with great information, but the chemistry between coach and player may not be there, which could make it difficult for the interactions to be productive. An instructor's ability does not hinge on what a player can comprehend and follow.

In other words, you could take a top-hitting coach from a major-league organization and ask them to teach a youth ball player, and the instructor may give them all the information they need in the simplest of ways possible. That player may *still* continue to have the same problems with their swing if their ability to absorb information from that coach isn't there.

Even players at the highest professional level of baseball and softball have personal hitting coaches that help them with their swing. This is no different than having a private tutor for a math course outside of regularly scheduled class time. One-on-one sessions undoubtedly offer more time for a hitter's unique issues to be addressed.

For the sake of time constraints, no player should expect their team coach to devote any significant amount of undivided attention to them during team practice. Team practice is for just that—the *team*. Things that involve individual needs should be addressed *outside* of practice and on the player's own time. Private time is to transform and fine tune the swing. Team practice usually serves as time for mass repetitions. There are also many team goals to be addressed during this time, leaving little room for players to think as much about their individualized issues.

Private instructors are there to help with any questions or concerns that are specific to you, so a hitter should not be afraid to ask for clarity if they don't understand something. If a hitter has been working with a particular trainer for a considerable amount of time, it's likely that the terminologies that the trainer uses will be easier and easier to follow as time goes on.

Terminology barriers between player and trainer can sometimes cause confusion if things are not clarified. This would include things like

"Rotate your hips."

"Drive your back side."

"Don't step in the bucket."

"Don't dip."

"Get inside the ball."

"Throw your hands."

"Get inside the ball."

MAXIMIZING YOUR TRAINING SESSIONS

Just like maximizing regularly scheduled team practices, a player can help solidify what was learned from a private training session much sooner than expected by taking the information that was learned from a session to recollect, ponder and analyze what took place. There are a few different methods that could be used that include the following.

- **Video Study and Analysis**

Using video analysis is great for giving the hitter an opportunity to *see* what he or she is doing during at-bats in the game or at hitting practice. With the accessibility to new technology today, it's very easy to be able to record a hitter's swing with just a press of a button. With mobile applications or PC software that allows you to edit and slow video down, it's a great way to keep track of progress.

This will force a hitter to look at their swing repeatedly to see if it matches up with what they *think* they are doing or comprehending as a hitter. Knowing how well they have been applying the information will help them gauge just how far they have to go to achieve the swing pattern they want.

- **Slow-Motion Drills**

Slow-motion drills will help players to not miss steps when improving their technique. Just like when kindergarteners first learn to tie their shoes, they don't do it very quickly on the first try. It takes a while before it feels natural. There is a similar process when it comes to hitting.

A hitter who expects to learn a new concept or technique at full speed on the first or second try is almost certainly asking for things to go wrong immediately and to be disappointed. This will only cause frustration in the learning process. When it's time to improve the swing, the number of *quality* repetitions is far more important than the *quantity* of repetitions.

Mirror drills go hand-in-hand with slow motion drills. A full-length mirror can be a hitter's best friend. It provides them an opportunity to *see* exactly what they are doing with their slow-motion swing *as* they do it. It gives the hitters a chance to see step-by-step what they are doing with their hands, hips, feet, etc.

- **Keeping a Hitter's Journal**

Part of being able to analyze your progress is having the ability to reflect. Reflection can be maximized by writing things down. You can tell a lot about a hitter who keeps a steady journal of their performances and thoughts. There is no easier way to track your own personal progress as a hitter than to flip the pages of your written journal and see some of the things you wrote down in the past like goals, things you wish to get a better understanding of, or new routines that you will do.

Writing things down will make your progress much more manageable and less overwhelming. It offers you an opportunity to connect with your own thoughts about your performance. Once you organize your thoughts, issues you may be having as a hitter will be much easier to resolve. Your goals become more real when you began to write them down and see them on paper. Transforming your thoughts and putting them on paper could be seen as the first step to making a vision becoming a reality.

There is no definitive way that a hitter has to compile their information for their journal. Since it's their own, they should take ownership and decide what *they* want to write and how they would like to go about it. However, a more productive and simplistic way of going about it would be to write a summary of the game or practice that took place. Write about as much as you can remember from your at-bats. Write about what you were thinking or feeling.

Were you hesitant?

Were you too anxious?

Were you feeling too arrogant?

Did you have a game plan for each at-bat?

Did you feel overmatched by the opposing pitcher?

Were you late with getting read on time for a swing?

Did you foul a ball off that you felt you should have crushed?

Writing goals down has been known to work wonders for the subconscious mind. After each game, sit down with a notepad or journal and try your best to remember every at-bat. Include what you did well and also what you wish you could have done better. If there was a pitch that you should have crushed, but you watched it go by for a strike without swinging, include it in your post-game notes.

Write down what you will do the next time someone throws you that pitch. Read it over and over and replay how you *want* the at-bat to go the next time. This is called mental rehearsal. Using visualization is a great tool to enhance preparation.

Use this writing process to *analyze*, not to *judge* yourself. Your reflection while doing your notes should be non-judgmental. While recollecting past mistakes, it's very easy to slip into a self-judgmental attitude. You may start to think negatively about who you are as a hitter, comparing yourself to other players who you think may be doing better or subconsciously telling yourself that you will never get to where you would like to be with your skill level. Be patient with yourself.

Recognize that the path to understanding your swing and what it takes to improve is a process that may take some time. Just be glad that you are taking the necessary steps to right your wrongs. The best part about keeping a personal hitting journal is that you don't have to show it to anybody if you don't want to. Tame your ego so that you can be *honest* with yourself in your reflection. You can't solve an issue that you don't first *truthfully* acknowledge.

Being honest with who you currently are as a hitter will help you to change for the better. It is okay to say, "I am not where I want to be with my two-strike hitting approach" or "I would like to be better with hitting change-ups." Some are hesitant to even think about what they need to improve on because it hurts their feelings to admit to themselves the areas that need improving.

- **Study Other Hitters**

Studying and analyzing the swing of other players can greatly help a hitter figure out their own flaws if it's done correctly. Seeing what works, what doesn't work, and picking out certain things that you think can be addressed help you become a better *thinking* hitter. When you watch someone else's swing, imagine what you would tell that hitter if you were asked for advice. Look closely for things that you can envision yourself telling them. What would you alert them to?

- Do they step too wide when they stride?
- Are they dipping their back shoulder?
- Are their hands not lined up correctly when they hold the bat?

You don't have to be an expert on hitting to do this exercise. This will help you connect the dots and start to come to your own conclusions about hitting. It will help you learn how to spot what works and what doesn't work based on the successes or failures of the hitter you are observing. The next step would be to actually *talk* to others and teach them about what you've learned on the subject.

- **Teaching Others**

    After becoming a private instructor, my understanding of hitting reached new heights. Once I was *forced* to fully analyze the swings of others, it opened up a new realm of understanding for me. This caused me to learn at a faster pace. It would most certainly do a hitter some good if they could take time to mentor, teach, or coach younger players. Perhaps you can volunteer to help someone in your neighborhood or a player on a younger team at your local ballpark.

    Teaching others in a hands-on manner helps create new ways of thinking about hitting. When you are tasked with helping someone else with their swing, it makes you rethink what you *really* know. Naturally, you will discover new ideas just from watching someone else closely and seeing how they implement the instruction that you are giving them. Do you have a younger brother or sister that plays as well? You could start with helping them. You can go to the backyard or to the local park and set up a hitting tee and just observe.

- **Using Real-Life Examples to Ingrain Information**

    Sometimes using outside references to drive a point home will help to further solidify a message. For instance, if you want to remember to start your swing with loading your hands back first, you can liken it to a person rearing back to throw a punch at a punching bag.

    Another individual may need to think of riding on a surfboard to help them remember to bend their knees in a way that will help them have a more athletic batting stance for good balance while hitting. These are just a couple examples. However, hitters can feel free to improvise and make up their own examples to remember proper form and technique.

One mental adjustment to a swing can help turn things around tremendously. Aside from a physical change in technique, the best way to help improve as a hitter is to enhance the *understanding* they have as a hitter first. A major part of mastering the art, science and philosophy of hitting is understanding how you can apply your knowledge of the information to help you produce results in the batter's box. Your ability to comprehend and apply what you know is the bridge between the information that is available out there and getting the results at the plate.

CHAPTER 4

POWER AND HITTING

Everyone is not built to hit the 450-foot-long bombs over the outfield fence. However, everyone *can* reach the full potential of the power that they are *capable* of achieving as a hitter within the parameters of their maximum capacity of strength. Oftentimes, hitters will try to overdo it on their swings in order to match the brute strength of another player. Attempting to compete with someone else's power without first paying attention to one's own natural ability will throw them off course and inhibit their ability to perform at their best.

To Swing Hard or Not to Swing Hard?

That is the question! A question that at times can be complex and could lead to many different answers. Oftentimes, players from little league and beyond are encouraged by coaches, parents, and others to *not* swing hard because it will make you lose control, or they tell them the opposite and to "swing hard so you can smack it."

Each bit of advice is usually given without much valid information to back up the command. It also doesn't take into account a player's skill level and where they are in their development as a hitter. There are plenty of myths that are spread around the baseball and softball community.

Many youth coaches will tell a player, "Don't swing out of your shoes! You'll lose control and balance!" which can be true in some cases, but the conversation usually ends there. What isn't being discussed, more times than not, is if whether or not the player is using the proper technique. If a hitter is not using the proper technique, then of course swinging with excessive force will cause all of the maladies in a swing to be exposed (i.e., off balanced or head "pulling off"). However, if a player is using the proper technique, a hard swing will not cause all of those things to happen.

HOW MUCH DOES HAVING POWER MATTER?

Can a player be a success at the plate without having power? In our world, the term "home run" is used to describe things that aren't even related to baseball. In general, people use the word as a means of describing something that was either successful or spectacular.

*"That movie was a **home run**!"*

*"Our new company project is going to be a **home run** with the corporate executives."*

So, this term alone represents enthusiasm and is synonymous with accomplishment. Looking at it this way, who wouldn't want to be a home run hitter? Surely anyone in their right mind would, right? But to those who truly *know* the game, they understand that there are many more ways to be successful at the plate than just hitting home runs or being known as a power hitter.

NO ONE CAN BE A BETTER YOU THAN YOU!

Problems can come about when a 9-hole hitter, last batter in the order, tries to adopt the mindset of being a home run slugger. This is not to be confused with somehow inadvertently convincing the batter to not have *confidence*. This is about making sure that as a hitter, you understand your capabilities and that you can still be a great contributor to the team by being the best in *your* capacity. That being said, there are ways that a hitter can improve their strength so that they can get the most out of what they are capable of producing, power-wise.

WAYS THAT HITTERS CAN INCREASE POWER

In general, when people discuss power in either baseball or softball, they are speaking about one of two things.

1. The hitter has strength based on muscular ability and body build.

2. The hitter has a technique that allows the ball to take optimal distance based on the backspin they can create, the extension they

get when driving through the ball or the trajectory they can cause the ball to take on its flight.

There are technical ways in which a hitter can improve their power involving form and technique, and then, there are physiological ways that players can improve their power involving muscular strength. It's quite obvious that in order for one to be successful as a hitter overall, it is ideal to be capable in both areas if possible. Strive to be both physically strong and be able to use technique to get the most power. You can ask a world-class bodybuilder to step into a batting cage and hit with power.

But we all know that just because they can lift 500 pounds doesn't mean that the same strength will translate into being able to hit a ball effectively. Perhaps they wouldn't even make contact because they haven't acquired the *skill* necessary to have the coordination or the hitting technique to use that strength productively. If it were that easy, you'd see bodybuilders all around the world trying out for professional baseball for a chance to make millions of dollars at the professional level.

On the flip side, you could take someone who knew *everything* about how to maximize power at the plate, but if they lack at least a minimal amount of kinesthetic power (physical strength), they won't accomplish much.

For example, taking a look at the wide range of body types among players at the professional level coupled with the differentiation in their performance's success, it's clear that the entire power discussion can be hard for some to figure out. You may see a very slim player who is leading the league in home runs or may tend to hit the ball further on a more consistent basis than other players who have a more muscular build. Usually, these types of players are just simply better at squaring the ball up at the right time and putting the right type of swing on it.

"Power is No Good Without Balance and Control."

With great power comes great responsibility. With great power in the batter's box, a hitter needs an even greater sense of discipline in order to *control* that power so that it doesn't hinder their performance. One might ask, "Well, how can power EVER be a bad thing?" Some players who become self-aware of their power in the batter's box at times could let it become a detriment because they expect *every* pitch they hit to be a bomb or a double off the wall. Some players who are known to have power can approach an at-bat with a mindset that says, "There can only be ONE outcome in this at-bat, and that's to knock the crap out of it. If that doesn't happen, I've failed!"

Of course, this could be a very subtle and subconscious message a power hitter can be replaying to themselves over and over. Where this can really hurt a team or batter is if the game situation requires them to be a little more strategic with their hitting approach as opposed to displaying their raw power. For instance, if there are less than two outs with a runner on third base and the infield is playing fairly deep, the hitter needs to focus on hitting the ball up the middle of the infield and on the ground in order to score a run from third base. If the hitter only focuses on hitting the ball as deep as they can, it may come back to harm the team. The hitter may hit a fly ball on the infield and get out because they couldn't control their urge to show off their power at the plate.

FINESSE

All power hitters must have the ability to tap into their *finesse* as a hitter. Your finesse as a hitter includes your ability to maneuver or handle the bat with a certain type of gracefulness and ease. This would be similar to how a basketball player needs to incorporate a certain degree of finesse to successfully complete a layup because using too much strength on a shot will make the ball bounce hard off the rim with no chance of going into the basket. A lack of finesse for a hitter and an inability to relax and let the swing have a certain degree of flow to it will result in a batter being rigid and stiff with their swing.

When your swing is rigid and stiff, it affects your bat speed. A stiff body cannot move as easily and as quickly as one that is more relaxed and loose. You can use examples from other sports as a means of truly understanding this concept.

The great martial arts master Bruce Lee was well known for his ability to properly balance both his quickness and power. He did it in a way that allowed him to deliver more impact in his punches and kicks even though he wasn't one of the biggest guys. Bruce Lee was fairly short with a very thin build but was able to throw a punch that would leave a bodybuilder in pain. In his teachings to his students, he emphasized that in order to operate efficiently in the practice of martial arts, one must envision their abilities like *water*.

He explained that you should strive to flow like water, being able to adjust to different situations in the same way that water adjusts to the shape of whatever objects it occupies (a cup, a pool, down a river in between rocks, etc.) while, at the same time, having the ability to exude power like a rolling tide in the ocean capable of engulfing anything in its path.

This analogy represents a great quality that all hitters should strive to exhibit in their hitting style—finesse. Having a level of finesse does not have to mean that you lack power, and having a certain level of power does not mean you have to lack finesse. The two characteristics do not always have to be mutually exclusive and are often dependent on one another. Since baseball and softball are thinking sports, power alone will *not* be sufficient enough.

How Would You Increase Power with Your Physical Strength?

Of course, technique is a huge portion of your swing path, extension, follow through, finish, etc., but what can a hitter do to increase their physical strength that will allow them to have a greater chance at maximizing their power?

Lower body exercises: a hitter's lower half is important for stability and of course hip rotation, etc. A simple list of leg exercises that would be great for hitters will include some of the following.

1. **Lunges**

2. **Squats**

3. **Squat jumps**

4. **Box jumps**

Core: The core is a very vital part of the swing as well. It's responsible for the twisting of the abdominal section during the swing. Good exercises for this part of the body include some of the following.

1. **Medicine ball twists:** You can do it with a partner standing back to back and passing the medicine ball to one another going clockwise, then reversing directions and going counterclockwise to work both sides of the abdominals and core.

If a player doesn't have a partner to work with, they can use a medicine ball to rotate as if they are mimicking a swing and throw the ball up against a sturdy wall made of concrete or into an open space where they have plenty of room.

2. **Planks**- This exercise forces an individual to use the core muscles to stabilize the body, which ultimately helps strengthen the core.

3. **Sit-ups and crunches**- old-fashioned, regular sit-ups and crunches are also beneficial to making sure that the core—the abdominals and obliques—are good and strong.

Forearms: Since the wrists are engaged during a good follow through on a swing, it's imperative to have strong forearms to help with the extension. Good forearm strength is an indicator of hand strength since the forearm muscles are responsible for the movement of the hands.

Hand Strength: Have you ever shaken the hand of someone bigger and stronger than you and you felt like your hand would crumble if they squeezed any tighter? Hand strength is a huge indicator of a person's *overall* strength. Hitters who have good strength in their hands are more likely to be able to have better control of the bat when they swing.

They also won't have as much give on their bats when they make contact with a pitch that is thrown harder. In other words, any ball they make contact with won't dominate the barrel of the bat on the swing, slow the bat down, or push it backwards when the hitter is attempting to extend through the ball. Coaches sometimes refer to this as "swinging a wet newspaper." If you envision this image, you'll understand. You also may hear the old saying "The pitcher knocked the bat out of his/her hand with that fastball." Hitters can prevent this from happening with hand and forearm strength training.

It's important to make sure that as a hitter, your swing is not interrupted by any fastball thrown by a pitcher. Hand strength will help ensure this. Hand strength can be built in just five minutes per day. With a stress ball in one hand and a timer in the other, you can create a regimen that will help improve your strength exponentially. For example, you could devise a plan to squeeze stress balls in each hand for one minute at a time. Doing two or three sets of this will be challenging at first, but with more and more repetitions, the hands and fingers will become much stronger, and you'll be able to build endurance for these drills.

The idea of power can activate a hitter's ego. Wanting to be the homerun hitter, awakening the urge to be the hero slugger on the team, and having all the attention associated with it are hard things for the hitter's ego to turn down. Instead of being the best *you*, the ego will convince you to be a hitter that pleases the superficial desires of others. It will make you want to impress everyone and abandon your technique that's best suited for you to succeed.

CHAPTER 5

SLUMPS

Having a single unsuccessful at-bat is one thing. Having a string of continuously unsuccessful at-bats is another. This extended series of strike outs, pop-ups, and weak groundouts is widely known as going through a slump. It's quite possibly the most dreaded, mentally torturing thing that a hitter can go through.

Even though the term is not exclusively used in baseball and softball, it's commonly associated with these sports. The term can of course be used for a basketball player whose free throw percentage has declined or for a golfer who can't find their swing.

Slumps are one of the hardest things to cope with for hitters of all ages. Short-term, they could range anywhere from three to five games. In some cases, even more! Some of the best baseball players in all of history have experienced *deep* slumps over their careers. All-time great New York Yankees player Derek Jeter had a streak in 2004 where he was zero-for-thirty-two at one point in the season.

That's right, ZERO hits in a span of thirty-two at-bats. He broke out of his slump with a homerun on the first pitch of the thirty-third at-bat. Afterwards, he was quoted saying "Pitchers aren't going to feel sorry for you. You've just got to go out and keep swinging," and continued, "It's a funny game sometimes." I believe the biggest thing to take away from what Jeter said is that you have to keep swinging. When a hitter adopts a defeated mentality, it lessens any chances of getting back on the right track.

WHEN THE SITUATION GETS DESPERATE

Desperation will make a hitter slip into a trance-like state and sometimes start doing things that aren't who they normally are as a hitter. For instance, they could be swinging at pitches they wouldn't typically swing at, or perhaps, they could be choosing to *not* swing at pitches that they *should*. All of this can sometimes happen without them even knowing *why* it is happening. Jokingly, it's almost as if a ghost takes over their body at the plate and makes decisions for them to swing at a pitch or watch it go by.

When hitters are struggling at the plate it can be from a combination of things. If they can't pinpoint exactly what it is, it can sometimes make things even more frustrating. It could be a mental thing. It may also be an issue with technique or proper form. It could be a little bit of both. Sometimes technique-based problems turn into mental slumps. For example, if a hitter has an issue with stepping out of the box during their swing and it affects their ability to connect well with the ball, it may lead to a mini-depression.

STEPS TO RECOVERING FROM A SLUMP

Slumps are inevitable. All players go through a period where they aren't performing as well as they could. This isn't anything for a player to feel *bad* about. As some of the best minds surrounding the sport have said very clearly, it's a part of the game. How you bounce back from a slump is what *really* defines a hitter. The goal is to in fact make sure that if you *do* encounter a slump, it doesn't last very long. Being able to detect the early symptoms of an oncoming slump might be able to keep a hitter from experiencing a slump that goes on too long.

1. USE YOUR HEAD. SWINGING HARDER ISN'T THE ANSWER.

Even though they won't admit it, players tend to get emotional when going through hard times at the plate. Embarrassment and frustration can be a heck of a thing to deal with especially when these growing pains are being witnessed by other people. To strike out over and over or to hit continuous ground balls and pop flies can eat away at one's self-esteem. Wondering what everyone else will think can also be a factor that weighs heavily on a hitter's mind. Feelings of *shame* can make a player feel even more defeated. If a hitter wants to recover quickly, they have to focus on the game itself and not the emotions that they are feeling as a product of their circumstances.

Don't swing harder; swing smarter!

2. DON'T TRY TO DO TOO MUCH.

There's an expression that a hitter is "trying to hit a 5-run homer." This of course isn't a real thing that a hitter can actually accomplish. But the adage suggests a hitter that is simply trying to do too much at once. Attempting to bite off more than you can chew will only lead to more and more disappointment. Attempting to correct all your wrongs with *one* swing will leave you even more frustrated. Coaches are known for saying, "Stay within yourself," which simply means to continue to strive to do what *you* are capable of doing.

When hitters get in slumps, many times they grip the bat a little tighter and their muscles tense up because they figure that it will somehow help.

Frustration turns to anger, and anger clouds the ability to think clearly. It also makes you do things that are not conducive to hitting well. Hitters should be aware of how their thoughts can work against them when dealing with frustration.

It may cause them to get more and more of what they don't want if they aren't aware of these things. It could make a player put the majority of their focus on negativity. The self-fulfilling prophecy is when a person says or believes something about themselves, good or bad, and that person takes actions to make their ideas of themselves come true.

3. GET HELP FROM OTHERS WHO *CAN* HELP.

A hitter in a slump is better off getting *qualified* help. This includes anyone who has had experience with helping players deal with slumps or who are well-versed in hitting. This person may be able to point out certain flaws in a swing or give advice on the best way to handle making adjustments to the swing. Finding a quality hitting coach or instructor is one of the best ways to make sure a hitter is getting what they need not only with the physical swing but the mental side of it also. The right information can do the trick in turning it all around. There may only be one or two key elements that a hitter needs to improve on to help take their game to the next level.

4. STAY PRESENT. FOCUS ON EACH MOMENT. BE IN THE "NOW."

Both baseball and softball each involve pitch-to-pitch game action. Each play starts with one pitch. All plays have a life of their own, unaffected by the last pitch before it or any pitch that is to come in the future. Regret and frustration from past at-bats will only fluster a hitter's mind and make it even harder to focus on their job at the plate during the at-bat.

5. REMEMBER YOUR PAST SUCCESS TO BUILD CONFIDENCE.

In most cases, thinking about the past can interfere with your focus on the present, but to *skillfully reflect* on something is different in many ways. When a player is in a position where they feel their performance is slipping, it can feel comforting to reflect on times that were better. This can remind them that they aren't as bad as they may perceive. This is a good way to get out of the mental funk and out from under the dark cloud of negative thoughts that come along with being in a slump.

Ultimately, what a hitter must understand is that even the best hitters have been in slumps on occasions. It's not indicative of whether you are a good or bad hitter. Slumps can end up just being temporary if you don't let them persist by letting negativity take over completely.

ADVICE FROM OTHERS

When a player is going through a slump, usually those who care about the player's situation will attempt to lend advice. Sometimes it's general advice and sometimes it's more specific advice if the individual is more qualified on the topic. It's in the hitter's best interest to at least hear *all* advice that is given, but for practical reasons, they cannot follow everyone's advice. Since information from different sources can be conflicting, to follow the advice of multiple, potentially conflicting sources could make matters even worse. The best approach would be for a hitter to consider all bits of assistance and then come to the best conclusion for themselves. Following the advice from others could make or break you.

A healthy dose of positivity and hope is the key ingredient to getting back on track. This helps fight off internalizing negativity. When you internalize a slump, you go from thinking,

"I am a *good* hitter experiencing bad times right now."

to thinking,

"I am a *bad* hitter. I may never get out of this slump."

With positivity and hope, a hitter will strive towards finding the right answer. With no hope of ever getting out of a slump, they may figure, "Oh well!" and deem it useless to even attempt to better the situation.

"This next at-bat can be the one that ends the slump!"

The above statement should be said repeatedly inside the hitter's head until the slump is over. Not only is it true, but it reminds the hitter that the end of the slump is right around the corner. Frustration from a slump leads to anger with the self *and* the situation. That anger leads to behaviors that can worsen results, which will only lead to even more frustration. Sadness usually follows frustration and anger. From mad-to-sad is a dynamic that happens many times when dealing with slumps.

Instead of trying to go five-for-five in the next game during a slump, strive to have *quality* at-bats. Focus on the following.

1. Picking good pitches to swing at.

2. Focus on being a good situational hitter.

3. Taking a base on balls if you need to.

What is most important is realizing that you don't have to be a hero *all* the time. Easing yourself out of a slump could be as simple as putting your focus on what you can do to help the team. Being a good team-oriented hitter is what counts. Being great at situational hitting is one of the most unselfish things that a hitter could strive for.

Situational hitting includes knowing who is on base, how many outs there are, and what you need to do to help advance base runners or score runs. Don't waste a failure. See them as opportunities and try your best to not let your mistakes happen more than once. All a hitter can do is try their very best to not make the same mistakes twice.

Former Major Leaguer, professional scout, and long-time performance coach for the Toronto Blue Jays Steve Springer is well-known for his philosophies on what a slump truly means to a player.

"Slumps are only for players who care about batting averages. To me, the batting average is Satan. Why? It's a trap. You can do everything right and still go 0-for-4. How could that be so? Well, you can hit four hard hit balls right at a player on the opposing team and get out each time. But, for that night your batting average is *zero*. Staring at a batting average of 0.000 could be enough to make a hitter completely lose all hope. Hitters should focus on *competing* rather than worrying about numbers and averages."

Adjusting one's mindset is the greatest challenge to those going through tough stretches.

"If hitters approach every game they play as if it were Opening Day, they would experience so much freedom. Everyone enters the new season full of optimism and hope for a good year. That all dies out once they experience some challenges early on, then it affects most of their at-bats in the future."

The key when going through a slump is to not try and do it all at once. The name of the game is to have a quality trip to the plate each time. Springer's list of characteristics of a quality at-bat consists of

1. A hard-hit ball.

2. Any hit, even though sometimes a hit can be a weak or "lucky." (As the old saying goes, "A blooper is a line drive in the scorebook").

3. Moving a guy over.

4. Any runs batted in (RBI).

5. A successful bunt.

6. A walk.

7. A hit-by-pitch.

8. An at-bat of eight pitches or more.

*You can learn more lessons from Steve Springer and about the mental approach to hitting at *qualityatbats.com*

Softball legend Laura Berg knows quite a bit about the ups and downs of hitting. She was a 4-time All-American in college, a 4-time Olympic gold medalist for the USA softball team, and later went on to be inducted into the Olympic Hall of Fame.

"In 2003, I went through a *horrible* slump. It seemed as if it didn't matter what I did, I just could not buy a hit. It was extremely frustrating. At the same time, I know that it was simply a part of the game. There were times where I would hit a laser at someone, but it was caught. There could be times where I would hit the ball off the end of the bat and it would go through for a base hit. At the end of your career it all evens out.

My advice to a hitter that is going through a slump would be to be more selective in the pitches you're swinging at. Usually when hitters are in a slump, they try to swing at almost everything as an attempt to dig themselves out of the hole. Remember to keep things as simple as you can."

CHAPTER 6

WHERE DO HITTERS GET THEIR CONFIDENCE?

Some hitters get their sense of confidence from past successes. For example, they may have had a previous game where they went four-for-four, and it boosted their self-image. Maybe they've been doing really well at their most recent practices or training sessions.

Confidence comes from knowing that you have what it takes to do what needs to be done at the right time. It's an internal trust that you have with *yourself*. It's about knowing that you have put in the work that will allow you to perform when it's game day.

There are those who know on a subconscious level that they aren't ready when they step into the batter's box because they didn't put in the work. This lack of readiness leads to anxiety. Anxiety makes it harder to focus on the task at hand. It makes a player think about things that don't have anything to do with the task in front of them. It can also cloud the mind with various, irrelevant mental gibberish and things to worry about that aren't connected with the hitter's agenda at hand.

What if I don't get a hit and break out of this slump?

What will my teammates think of me if I strike out AGAIN this game?

Will the coach bench me if I don't hit well this game?

Am I going to embarrass my parents if I don't get a hit in this at-bat? The car ride home is going to be dreadful!

So how can they concentrate on a task with such obsessive thought patterns? Well, quite simply, they can't! Usually hitters who think like this have no choice but to rely on a bit of luck to succeed in their at-bats, hoping that they will swing at the right time and that the bat is on the right swing plane with the pitch so that they can connect. Having this kind of mindset will put a hitter at a disadvantage. In both baseball and softball, the team that is hitting is recognized as the *offensive* team and the ones in the field, including the pitcher, is acknowledged at the defensive side. However, is a hitter really on the *offensive*, in their approach and strategy, if they are using the *defensive* mindset that is more *reactionary* than *proactive*?

How do you get rid of nervousness and anxiety so that you can operate with confidence in the batter's box? Building the trust in yourself is the major key! When you study hard for a test, you feel prepared and ready to get a high grade. However, if you know that you *haven't* been studying as much as you should, you may feel a tad bit nervous when you sit down to take the test because you don't trust that you will know all of the answers.

Treat your hitting practice as if you're studying for a test, which is game day. When you step into the batter's box with your bat in your hand ready to hit, that's equivalent to you sitting down at the desk of a classroom with a pencil in hand, ready to answer test questions. In both instances, if you aren't truly ready, it will show.

WHAT'S THE DIFFERENCE BETWEEN BEING CONFIDENT AND BEING COCKY?

This game is one that has a very interesting way of humbling those who think they have mastered it. Plenty of players have gone four-for-four in one game and then went zero-for-four in the very next. It's a game where you have to remain *balanced* in your thoughts. This means not thinking too highly or too lowly of yourself. You have to live by the saying, "You're not as good as you think you are, but you're also not as bad as you think you are." This is the happy medium that is necessary.

High-level hitting is a constant mental game with YOURSELF. When you step into the box, it's a solo mission. Only *you* can swing that bat that you hold in your hand. No matter what your parents, teammates, or coaches think about you, it is *you* that controls the outcome at *that* moment. No one can swing at a bad pitch for you. No one can get you off balance. No one can make you look at a good pitch right down the middle of the plate without swinging at it.

Some may find a lot of pressure in the notion that it's all on them as an individual, but this also is a very beautiful and liberating idea because this gives *you* all of the true power. No one else can interfere with your at-bat. It's not the same as a sport like football, where the wide receiver has to rely on a good throw from the quarterback for them to do their job of catching the ball. For the most part as a hitter, no teammate can interfere with your success. There may be rare instances where a teammate doesn't execute on a hit and run or a bunt play, but the pitcher-hitter battles are an individual mission.

THE "SO WHAT?" PHILOSOPHY

So, let's say you strike out. Now what?

Are you embarrassed?

Do you not care?

Are you angry?

Are you frustrated?

Do you want to break down and cry?

Have you thought about the worst that can happen when you don't perform well at the plate? Anxiety comes when a player is worrying about what will happen in the future. This is what causes the disease of unease.

"What will happen if I *don't* do well?"

That's the main question on the minds of most hitters, if not on a conscious level, then most definitely on a deeper *subconscious* level. Some hitters dread the negative "what-ifs" so much that it's *all* that they can think about when they are in the batter's box. It seems crazy, right? Instead of focusing on moment to moment, pitch to pitch, they are too busy thinking about what will happen if they *don't* succeed in the at-bat. This robs them of their concentration. The most powerful form of concentration one has is their attention to the *present*.

This why a mentally tough hitter should skillfully adopt the "so what" attitude as a valuable asset. This doesn't mean that they do not care for their performance. It just means that they have learned how to detach their performance from their character and who they are. If you have an at-bat where you don't succeed, would that mean that you are any less of a person? Does that mean that you aren't a worthy individual? The answer is "no" to each of these questions.

The "so what" approach isn't to say,

"So, what! My performance doesn't matter at all. Why should I even try?"

It's to say, *"So, what! I didn't accomplish my goal of getting a hit <u>this time</u> around, but you know what? Next time I will be ready. I'll make sure of it!"*

With a positive attitude comes great confidence. In fact, it's sometimes a positive attitude that makes way for the confidence to build in the beginning process. You don't need to have seen yourself perform well in the past in order to be positive about your future performances. In the beginning, all you need is the *belief* that things can get better. Those who take this notion to the next level won't just say they believe things will get better, but they will have the attitude the they *know* things will get better.

Hitters have to incorporate just enough "so what" in their mindset so that it doesn't deflate them if they happen to not succeed in an at-bat. I knew of a player who took a permanent marker and in big, bold, capital letters wrote "So what?" as a reminder not to get too low when things didn't go their way. Every time they would strike out, hit a lazy fly ball for an out, or produced a weak grounder on the infield, they'd take their helmet off and look at the "So what?" that they had written underneath the bill of the helmet as a reminder.

Explore "Chapter 2: Quality vs. Quantity" again to understand why that is a key essential to building the confidence needed. A player knows deep down when they've had more than enough empty practices filled with lollygagging and daydreaming. They may have taken a hundred swings, but none of them were done with focus, concentration, or attention to detail. Don't cheat yourself. Hitters should spend their time *wisely* when working on their swing.

Out of the 168 hours in a week, only a small percentage of that is going to be devoted to swinging a bat. Not necessarily because the hitter doesn't want to work hard but because of the fatigue on the body. The arduous effort of swinging prevents hitters from taking too many repetitions in any given training session, which is another one of the main reasons why quality over quantity is preached. Too many swings will make a hitter lose their form and technique due to fatigue. This is how bad habits are formed. A solid half-hour of focused, concentrated, quality hitting goes a long way in comparison to an hour long of swinging without a purpose.

Swing with a Purpose

The body learns through muscle memory. No matter if you take a good or bad swing, the body's memory is always recording its movements. Therefore, swinging with a *purpose* is key in both practices and games.

"BASEBALL IS THE GREATEST SPORT BECAUSE IT ALLOWS SOMEONE LIKE ME (MODERATELY TALENTED) TO COMPETE AT THE HIGHEST LEVEL AGAINST MUCH MORE PHYSICALLY TALENTED PLAYERS BECAUSE IT IS MUCH MORE MENTAL THAN THE OTHER SPORTS."

GREG LITTON

CHAPTER 7

POSITIVE THINKING

You'll never hear an accomplished hitter say that negative thinking has ever helped them in their efforts to become an elite hitter. This is because there is nothing about negativity that could ever help a player achieve success at the plate. Therefore, a hitter should never engage in negativity in any form. That includes thought, speech, or action. Negativity of any type, will only put unsureness and hesitation in a batter's mind, both of which will make a hitter less likely to be confident in themselves.

THOUGHT (AFFIRMATIONS, PAST THOUGHTS, AND ANTICIPATION)

Thought comes *before* action in most cases. Before *doing* positive things, you must *think* positive thoughts about the things you wish to do. The more positively a hitter feels about themselves, the more likely it is that they will be more ready to capitalize on positive opportunities when they present themselves.

If positive thinking were as easy as people made it seem, people would not have such a hard time fighting off their negative thoughts. Of course, being a positive thinker is one of the hardest things to do for athletes at times, especially if they haven't been performing too well. Imagine striking out three times in a single game and then trying your best to remain positive amidst all of the shame, embarrassment, and disappointment you may feel. There is no doubt that hitting a moving ball delivered from a pitcher is one of the hardest things to do in all of sports.

SPEECH: WHAT YOU SAY TO OTHERS AND WHAT YOU SAY TO YOURSELF

What you say is a portrayal of what's on your mind. How you *speak* about your recent circumstances at the plate is a sign of whether you are thinking negatively or positively about your situation. Never voice negativity about your performance. Use your words carefully. How you train your *subconscious mind* through your thought, speech, and actions will determine how you will operate on a daily basis.

The <u>subconscious mind</u> is one of the most powerful things a person possesses, yet it is severely overlooked and underestimated. It goes unnoticed because it is the part of your mind that runs under the surface of your forethought, and you're completely unaware of it when you're awake. Since psychologists have proven that a person's subconscious is responsible for a vast amount of activity in behavior, it's essential that a player understands what kind of power it holds and how to use it to their advantage. Your subconscious is what allows for you to memorize a song that you only heard a couple of times on the radio, without really trying to remember it. Your subconscious is like a tape recorder that never turns off. It sees and hears things that your conscious mind doesn't even notice. So, a player's subconscious mind is operating off of what it hears, not just from others, but from what it hears the player say about themselves.

ACTION: BODY LANGUAGE AND HOW YOU CARRY YOURSELF

A huge part of remaining positive is the body language you exude. You often can look at a player's preparation in the on-deck circle and see whether they have some confidence. Their overall swagger might give away the fact that they truly believe in themselves and their abilities. On the contrary, a slouched back with a head hanging low can tell a rather different story.

This may sound strange and creepy to some, but when you're not in a confident mood or feeling too sure of yourself because you may be feeling anxious, you should smile. That's right, smile! Put a big grin on your face, even if it's for a quick moment. Scientists have studied the emotional connection between a smile and a person's mood. Since a smile usually follows a good feeling that a person has, the same dynamic can work in reverse. A smile can cause a good feeling in a person, even when they don't have anything good to feel about.

The body's physiology works in mysterious ways. If you're in doubt, experiment with this on your own. Whenever you're feeling nervous or in doubt about your performance, smile, and you will see that it almost *instantly* forces your mood to change. It's very hard to smile *and* be frustrated, angry and worried. Don't think about how you will look to others. It may be hard to force a smile, but it will certainly help get your mind back on the right track—to positivity.

Repetition is the mother of all learning—repetitive thoughts, repetitive speech, and repetitive actions. Bad habits on repeat will cause a player to learn in a negative fashion. Good habits on repeat will cause a player to learn things that will send them in a more positive direction.

"Repetition is key" is a long-time cliché', but the *type* of repetition is most important.

CLEARING YOUR MIND BEFORE AN AT-BAT

One of the hardest things to do in softball or baseball is to clear your mind and *focus* during your at-bat. Usually, there are many things to distract us from the task at hand. From what happened last inning, to the fact that your team is losing by a large margin, the homework you have due tomorrow morning, or what you feel like eating after the game, our minds can be very busy with chitter-chatter.

It's like our minds have a background noise at all times that could distract us at any second, yanking and pulling at our consciousness to pay attention to whatever it has playing in the background. Many players bring the memory of old, outdated at-bats that happened a while ago to the plate with them each time they go up to hit. Carrying old mental baggage will certainly weigh you down.

All plays that happen...
happen in the present.

One of the chief obstacles of remaining in the present moment when hitting is occupying your mind with the past or worrying too much about what will happen in the future. You may have struck out your first at-bat of the game. That could affect every following at-bat for the rest of the game, *but only if you let it*. If you treat each pitch as if it has a life of its own, it will help in staying more present-minded. The previous pitch cannot have a physical effect on any following pitches even though, strategically, the number of balls and strikes changes from pitch to pitch, which will determine what a hitter's approach will be.

The Chattering Mind

This is when a player's thoughts run rampant with the little to no control of what comes in or out of their thought process.

Here are some ways to tame the chattering mind in your head before an at-bat.

1. Take deep breaths.

2. Practice your focus while on deck.

When the human body takes deep breaths it helps to ease anxiety, which some players have plenty of before at-bats because their minds are thinking of a million different outcomes at once.

"Will I get out?"

"Am I going to pop up again?"

"I hope I hit a homerun. I want to impress everyone at the game."

These are just a few intrusive thoughts though there are a myriad of things that one could be thinking about, but slow deep breaths can help ease these thoughts. Counting while breathing could help even more. Count on the inhale and then count on the exhale. While doing this, it's hard to also think about all of the other thoughts that don't matter.

Breathing in: "One, two, three, four, five…"

Breathing out: "One, two, three, four, five…"

Hitters will have seemingly countless at-bats in their careers. This means they currently have many past at-bats, many that lie ahead in the future or perhaps both. Superior-minded hitters can't allow themselves to be affected by things that have already happened or things that they anticipate *might* happen in the future. Either will distract them from their goals of the present.

Remaining present takes practice. If hitters aren't used to playing in a present state of mind, it might be difficult in the beginning. But like anything involving developing skills, it takes practice to improve. Therefore, they should work on their present-minded focus. When they are at team practice, instead of daydreaming while they are going through hitting drills, they should focus on each and every swing one at a time.

They must make a conscious decision to drown out all other thoughts out and concentrate on each swing. If a hitter does this consistently at practice, they will develop a better ability to focus their minds in the present and during games.

Positive thinking makes hitters more confident, but that should never be mistaken as a green light to be arrogant or cocky. No matter how confident a player becomes or how well they improve on their hitting, they must always aim to increase their skills. Improvement is not a sign that a hitter should stop working hard. *Maintaining* batting skills can be just as demanding as attaining them. In this case, it's a matter of working hard to get it and even harder to keep it.

A piece of humble pie is just around the corner once you think you've mastered it. Always live by the motto

"*You are never as bad as you think you are and you're never as good as you think you are.*"

Positive thinking hitters keep focused on what they *do* want, not what they *don't* want. Going to the plate and thinking, "Don't strike out! Don't strike out! Don't strike out!" will cause you to only think about doing exactly that—striking out. Positive thinking may be something that doesn't necessarily come easily. Therefore, it could take some practice to get used to it. Just like any other habit, consistent positive thinking takes time to form. Practice having positive thoughts on a daily basis, and it will come more easily every time.

"SLUMP? I AIN'T
IN NO SLUMP, I
JUST AIN'T
HITTIN'"

YOGI BERRA

CHAPTER 8

UMPIRES

U mpires are not some sort of new species that come from another planet that is light years away. Believe it or not, they are living, breathing, thinking human beings just like you are. They are susceptible to making mistakes just like you. Some umpires are better than others. But to be honest, none of this matters because you can't control any of these things. You won't be able to select which umpire is behind the plate when you step into the box. You can't control whether they are having a good or bad strike zone. They may get mad at your coach and decide to start giving calls in favor of the other team. That, too, is something that you won't be able to control.

So, how should you deal with umpires?

While there aren't a lot of things that you *can* do to influence an umpire to your benefit, there are lists of things that you *don't* do for certain.

1. Do not challenge an umpire in the middle of an at-bat with your *body language*. For example, let's say that you have one strike against you during an at-bat. The umpire yells, "Strike two!" on the next pitch, and you disagree that the pitch was in the strike zone. Then, you turn around, roll your eyes at the umpire, and let out a big sigh in disbelief.

   This is something you most definitely do not want to do unless you want to get on the umpire's bad side for the rest of the game. It also may make things harder for your teammates because you are a representative for your team by how you carry yourself on the field. Even though umpires aren't expected to hold grudges and give bad calls based on personal grudges on players, they still can do it without it being noticeable or without anyone being able to dispute it with real evidence.

2. Do not challenge an umpire with your *words*. Even if you believe you are doing it in the most polite way possible, it's best to not speak. Not exactly because it's the wrong thing to do, but because it *could* be interpreted as the wrong thing. You are responsible for what you say, but you have no control over how umpires interpret what you say.

    So, it's best to just play the game with your lips sealed to the umpire while you are hitting. You may get a strike called on you, and for the sake of knowing how to gauge the strike zone in your next at-bat you may ask the umpire, "Blue, where was that pitch?" You may ask with a genuine sincerity, but it may come across as you having an attitude. Regardless, it's best to not leave things up for interpretation.

3. Do not challenge an umpire with *laughing* in a condescending manner. When you do things like this, it makes the umpire feel as if you believe they are a joke. It also makes you appear to have a bad attitude, which if you are being scouted by potential colleges or recruiters, will be one of the quickest ways to become a turn off. A supreme hitter must carry themselves with the utmost integrity.

When it comes to umpires, being an attentive observer in the dugout and in the on-deck circle is your best bet. See where the umpire is calling ball and strikes; then, adjust accordingly. A hitter that pays attention to these things will at least have a better idea of where *umpire's* strike zone is. If the umpire has an expanded strike zone, one that is "stretched" or bigger than the average umpire's, it allows the hitter to be prepared to swing at pitches that may be borderline of the strike zone.

Never allow yourself to believe that you will be at a disadvantage because of a good or bad umpire. It will only take away from your focus and concentration. Hitters should focus on controlling the things that they *can* control and nothing else. Don't make yourself out to be a victim of an umpire, even when you may feel that an unfair call has been made. If you're lucky enough to have a long career, you will notice that you will have plenty of at-bats in which you feel like the umpire's strike zone favors the opposing pitcher.

Umpires have a job and so do you. Do not allow yourself to pick and choose how well you will do your job based on how they do theirs. Disagreeing on a bad call is a part of the game. You do not have to be happy about who is standing behind the plate, but you have to maintain a sense of respect for them no matter what. Those who carry themselves in a professional manner at all times, as all superior hitters should, will rarely have an issue with umpires during games.

"The best compliment
you can give a hitter
is that he's a tough
out; that initiates
fear in a pitcher."

Billy Butler

CHAPTER 9

SITUATIONAL HITTING

S ituational hitting isn't exactly seen as the coolest subject to talk about in the eyes of most hitters. Often, it entails giving yourself up for the team. Essentially, situational hitting is sacrificing your own success so that the team can succeed. However, if you see situational hitting as a win-win situation as opposed to a lose-win situation, you will be a much more effective situational hitter. It takes a special kind of team player with a "team first" mentality to be great at situational hitting. Situational hitting is exactly what it sounds like—the ability to hit in accordance with whatever game situation is current.

Situational instances may include:

1. Sacrifice Bunt.

2. Hit-and-run play.

3. Hitting a ground ball to the right side of the infield to move a runner from second to third base.

4. Hitting a ground ball to middle infield to score a runner from third base with less than two outs.

5. Hitting a sacrifice fly ball to the outfield to score a runner from third base with less than two outs.

6. Not swinging at a pitch, even if it's a strike, when a teammate has a good jump on a steal to prevent a dead ball situation with a foul ball.

Being a good situational hitter takes having a more heightened awareness than the average player. You must assess the situation as it is shaping out before you even step to the plate. While on deck, a hitter should be observing the scene and weighing the circumstances by analyzing what inning the game is in, the score, the type of pitcher, the part of the lineup up to bat, the speed of the runners on base, what bases are occupied, etc. Any bit of information that could factor into the outcome of the game should be considered.

HITTING WITH TWO STRIKES

One of the most common situational hitting instances is when hitters have two strikes on them in an at-bat. Some hitters don't make an adjustment to the pitch count, which is a sign that a player is not yet privy to situational hitting. It is not valuable to have the same approach with two strikes as when the hitter has no strike or one strike.

Mental toughness and determination are keys to being a great hitter that is hard to strike out. Being someone who is hard to strike out should be a characteristic that a player takes extreme pride in. Good two-strike hitters tend to have higher batting averages overall compared to those who are more likely to strike out. Knowing that you can do what it takes to get the job done with two strikes will give you a lot of confidence and allows you to be more relaxed early in the count. Those who feel that they are not as good at two-strike hitting may feel anxious and force things to happen early in the pitch count just to avoid having to deal with the possibility of striking out deeper in the count.

Some hitters would rather just make contact early, regardless if they get a good pitch to swing at, because they are *terrified* of getting into a two-strike situation. If a player has the right attitude, confidence and knowledge, they won't be afraid of the two-strike situation, and they will decrease the amount of bad pitches that they swing at.

Here are some key characteristics that a good two-strike hitter must have to be successful

- Is a true competitor
- Lacks fear
- Has a sense of "fight" in them (an absolute refusal to go down looking on a ball near the strike zone)
- Follows the idea of "When in doubt, foul it out" (of play). Even if they have to foul a pitch off to survive the at-bat, they will do so.

HITTER'S COUNT

Knowing when you're in a hitter's count is important because it gives you an edge over the pitcher. In general, a hitter's count is any pitch count that is in the favor of the hitter because the pitcher is behind in the count and is forced to throw a strike to avoid walking the batter. These are counts like:

Balls	Strikes
1	0
2	0
3	0
3	1

In a hitter's count, the batter should *not* swing at pitches that are not clearly in the strike zone. It may even mean that they should allow a strike to go by if it is placed on the corner of the strike zone where it is difficult to make good contact with the ball. For example, if a hitter is in a 2-0 count and the pitcher delivers a strike that is low in the strike zone and covers the very edge of the plate, would it be a good pitch to swing at? A batter very well *could* get a hit on a pitch like this. But would it be the smartest thing to do when you know what the chances are? Would it be the smartest thing to do knowing that the pitcher could potentially throw you something *much* better during the at-bat?

A general rule of thumb is that hitters are expected to swing harder on hitter's counts. Since they are in less of a defensive mode, this allows them to let loose a little more. With two strikes, the mentality changes, and hitters are expected to put the ball in play by making contact in any way possible, preferably a line drive or, at the very least, a ground ball. Avoiding pop ups is the usual protocol, but when making contact with two-strikes, it is very important.

KEYS TO MAKING ADJUSTMENTS

Hitters that are incapable of adjusting during a season, during a practice, during a game, or during an at-bat will not succeed at the level they are capable of. Making pitch-by-pitch adjustments may be much more difficult than making them at-bat to at-bat. Making a change to my approach at the plate is done much easier if I've had a couple of innings to think about what I did wrong in my first at-bat so that I can shift my focus in my second at-bat.

However, if during an at-bat I get fooled on an off-speed pitch (curveball, changeup, or anything other than a fastball) and swing off-balanced, I should make it a point to stay back on the next pitch and not get fooled again. This would be a quick adjustment that would have to take place within a span of less than twenty seconds or so.

TAKING WHAT THE PITCHER GIVES YOU

Hitting coaches are infamous for telling hitters to use the whole field. What this really means is that a batter should have the ability to hit the ball to left field, centerfield, or right field according to *where* the pitcher throws the pitch (i.e. inside or outside). Young players, especially, have a habit of attempting to pull every ball they hit during training and practice. Nothing says undisciplined hitter like a player working on pulling almost every single ball in tee work, in soft toss or in batting practice.

The very reason why pitchers at higher levels aim to throw the ball toward the outside corner of the plate is because most people know that the average hitter does not have the correct approach to be able to utilize the whole field. These pitchers instinctively know that a mediocre hitter won't have the appropriate mindset of using the whole field and will struggle with outside pitches. Knowing this information, all hitters should be on a mission to counter these pitches by enhancing their ability to hit the ball to all parts of the field when needed.

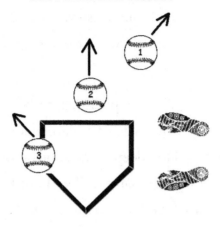

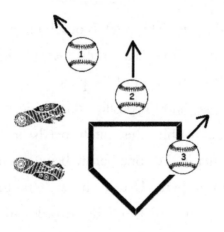

Ball #1: Inside Pitch

Ball #2: Middle Pitch

Ball #3: Outside Pitch

These two diagrams, depicting both a right- and a left-handed hitter, show where a hitter should make contact with each corresponding pitch.

- _Inside pitch:_ This pitch has to be hit out in front of the plate. If a player allows a pitch to travel too deep in the zone on the inside, they will get "jammed" and not be able to connect the barrel with the ball. They will instead be more likely to connect with the handle.

- _Middle pitch_: This pitch is best hit right at the front of the plate right before the ball crosses the front of the plate.

- _Outside pitch_: Typically, the hardest of all three to hit, this pitch needs to travel further in the zone before being connected with properly. Usually, hitters tend to stick their bats out too early in order to make contact with this pitch, which can cause them to get off balance and put a weak swing on the ball. Players tend to hit the ball on the end of the bat if they attack an outside pitch out in front of the plate.

Most players are naturally inclined to pull the ball. The average person can close their eyes and swing a bat with one hand and manage to hit it on their pull side by default. It takes discipline and a steady approach to be able to be a great all-around hitter. A hitter may be in a game situation where there is a runner on base who needs to be advanced to the next base. The lack of ability to use the whole field might cost them, for example, as there are times when a right-handed hitter has to hit a ball on the ground to the right side of the infield in order to move a runner from second to third base.

SWITCH-HITTING

Those who have developed the ability to hit from both sides of the plate have a distinct offensive advantage. The rewards offered to the switch hitter include being able to avoid pitches that break *away* from the hitter like sliders and curveballs. Switch hitting is more common in baseball than it is in softball, although many softball players learn to hit left-handed in order to have the advantage of *slap hitting,* which means getting a running lead to first while still in the batter's box and able to put a swing on the ball. Some well-known players have been hitting and perfecting their swing from both sides from an early age. Others have decided later in their careers that they would like to add this ability to their repertoire.

For those who make the decision later, the *why* and the *how* are the two questions that stand out immediately.

- *Why would anyone want to switch-hit?* Curveballs, sliders, and cutters are pitches that move away from hitters based on the rotation and spin of the ball that these types of pitches produce. They make for some of the toughest pitches to hit. To avoid having to deal with the difficulties associated with them and to make hitting more consistent, the handedness of the pitcher will dictate from which side the batter will swing.

(When facing a left-handed pitcher, players will hit right-handed, and when pitchers are right-handed, players will hit left-handed).

- *How would a player begin learning how to hit from their non-dominant side if they ever wanted to start?* Those looking to start switch-hitting later in their career may experience difficulties and frustrations with learning how to duplicate the timing, rhythm, and coordination on the other side. We tend to be more coordinated in one hand than the other. Of course, this is the reason why people brush their teeth, write, use scissors and a plethora of other things with one dominant hand.

It appears to be stronger, but this is not always the case. We simply have a greater ability to complete sophisticated movements with one hand over the other. Most people are right-hand dominant. Most hitters in the world are right-handed to reflect this. When hitting, most of the time, the dominant hand is the one on top.

The reason why it may be a challenge when switching around to the opposite side of the plate is because the hitter's less coordinated hand is now the one on top when gripping the bat. Naturally, the top hand is the hand that is used to control the bat and push through the swing to provide the power.

Another challenge to switch hitters who are making the adjustment is that their lead eye has changed. For right-handed hitters, their lead eye is their left eye, which is the closest to the pitcher. Years and years of getting used to tracking a pitch with this eye as the primary eye to focus on the ball is something key to understand and overcome.

Here are a couple of ways that a hitter could work on enhancing their coordination and skill from their non-dominant side.

1. <u>One-Hand Drill</u>: Use your top hand on your less coordinated side to hit off of the batting tee or during soft toss. For example,

someone who is attempting to learn to hit left-handed should hold the one-hand bat in their left hand while taking swings during these drills. One-hand bats are sold everywhere that baseball equipment is purchased. However, some hitters use very small and light tee-ball bats as a substitute.

2. <u>Feet Together or "No Step/No Turn" Drill</u>: When refraining from stepping with the front foot or using the hips, a hitter can solely work on the movement and coordination of the hands when they place their feet together and focus on a "hands only" approach. To visualize this, imagine a golfer with their feet closely together and getting ready for a putt. Players are surprised when they find out how difficult this can be. It requires an incredible amount of bat control and discipline. It's a drill that exposes a lot of defects in the swing, even from the dominant side.

Some players have even been known to think outside the box and use more quirky methods of improving fine motor skills and dexterity by brushing their teeth or writing the alphabet with their weaker coordinated side to work on the smaller muscles of the hand and arm in order to build more sophisticated movement ability.

The most important takeaway from all of this is that if a hitter truly wants to take a shot at learning how to hit from their less dominant side, there are methods and steps to make it a reality. The road to succeeding from the non-dominant side may be difficult, but it is very possible depending on how dedicated one is to learning the skills necessary.

TAKING ONE FOR THE TEAM

One of the hardest things for any player to do is to stand in a batter's box and allow a wildly thrown hard ball to hit them on the legs, ribs, shoulders, or forearms. Top athletes of other sports have reflected on how they were once baseball or softball players but could not deal with even the thought of being hit with a ball traveling at such high speeds. This is enough to make some individuals want to quit. It takes a special type of mentality to allow yourself to get hit to get on base for the betterment of your team. One of the biggest sins at the plate is jumping out of the way of a pitch so that you can spare yourself of the pain of being hit, especially if it's during a situation where the team truly needs baserunners.

At the higher levels of the sport, college recruits and professional scouts see it as a sign of weakness and lack of being team-oriented if a player is quick to jump out of the way of a pitch. But one who can stand in the batter's box and tuck their front arm elbow into their body and *safely* turn their heads away from the direction of the pitch and take one for the team will be the ones who stand out in the minds of recruiters or scouts. This is also something that helps a batter earn the ultimate respect from teammates.

Note: Keep in mind that this is most suitable when a hitter has less than three balls on them in the pitch count. If a ball is thrown out of the strike zone for a ball four, this is a case where it wouldn't matter if the batter stayed in the box or not.

CORRECT   **INCORRECT**

CHAPTER 10

HOW TO BE AN ON-DECK
SCIENTIST

In order to be a more complete hitter, you must be able to inspect a pitcher from the on-deck circle. It's critical to be ready for good pitches when you get them. If not, you could end up wasting an at-bat and being frustrated when you're not ready for certain pitches. A good hitter is known to take advantage of mistakes that pitchers make like fastballs down the middle of the plate or hanging curve balls that don't quite curve.

To fully study a pitcher, you have to know what it is you are looking for. Here are some key details for hitters to pay attention to in order to make the most out of their at-bats:

1. Velocity

2. Arm slot

3. Pitch count tendencies

Velocity is important to a hitter and should be focused on because it will impact the hitter's timing. With timing being such a crucial element to any batter's swing, it's important to take note of how fast or slow a pitcher is throwing. This will be relative to age of the players and level of competition. In the lower age groups, pitchers do not throw a wide variety of pitches, so hitters in the on-deck circles don't need to be concerned about anything other than how fast or how slow the pitch is thrown. When players reach the higher levels of the game, the concern of what *type* of pitches are being thrown is imminent.

Arm slot is also a major factor because it involves how well a hitter is able to *see* pitches. The arm slot, or angle, that the ball comes out of the pitcher's hand when being delivered to the plate will determine the angle of the ball when leaving the mound.

Pitch count tendencies are a more intricate part of the game that require a more comprehensive knowledge of baseball/softball to understand. Although it's not rocket science, it does take more knowledge of the game to comprehend while on-deck. A more simple example of a hitter determining pitch count tendencies would be a hitter noticing that an opposing pitcher always throws a curveball when the count is 1-1.

A more complex tendency to recognize could be a pitcher who delivers different types of pitches depending on how their rhythm is with their wind up. For example, a pitcher that slows down their delivery to the plate may be giving away the fact that they are about to throw a changeup or perhaps another type of off-speed pitch. That same pitcher, when throwing a fastball to the plate, may quickly go through their pitch delivery.

UMPIRE TENDENCIES

Not only do you have to keep an eye on the habits of the pitcher, but it may do you some good to have an idea of what type of umpire you have behind the plate when on deck. No two umpires are exactly alike. Some have strike zones as wide as the ocean and others have a smaller strike zone that's tighter than most.

The time spent in the on-deck circle shouldn't be used to see who is in the stands watching the game or to goof around with teammates that are in the dugout. Use this as valuable *study time.* After all, the hitter on deck will never know how many pitches the hitter in front of them will see. What if they only get to work on their timing for one pitch because the batter ahead of them swings at the first pitch they see and puts the ball in play?

This also brings up the subject of why it's important to try and see what the opposing pitcher is doing when you are in the hole, third batter in line to hit or even if you're the fourth batter in line to hit. Players can keep track of mostly the same observations of the pitcher while in the dugout as they can when they are in the on-deck circle.

As always, clear your mind by taking deep breaths while in the on-deck circle. Being able to control your breathing will help you to relax.

"HITTING IS TIMING, PITCHING IS UPSETTING TIMING."

WARREN SPAHN

CHAPTER 11

WHAT IS YOUR JOB IN THE BATTING ORDER?

All hitters should seek to do as best as they can, no matter what position they are assigned in the batter order. For some, the batting lineup is an indicator of talent level and capability. At the higher levels of the game, the placement of players within the lineup becomes strategically important. In a hitter's career, they may be asked to hit in a spot in the order that they do not agree with. However, being disappointed at where the coach places you in the lineup is a waste of time and energy. A hitter's focus must immediately turn to what they can do to be the best they can be in the role that they were asked to fill in that game, for that inning, and for each pitch.

The main objective of every hitter is, of course, to produce when they are at the plate, to get on base, and to eventually score. However, the expectations and role for each hitter in the lineup may vary. If you are not satisfied with your placement in the order, it's best to *fight* for the spot you feel you deserve.

LEADOFF HITTER

In the order, this spot is a special one. It's the first batter in the order, which means they are expected to be the ones to get the offense started. Their mentality must be to get on base *by any means necessary*. Here are some characteristics that lead-off hitters are known to traditionally have

1. Usually above average speed.

2. Patient and has the ability to pick out good pitches to hit.

3. Good contact hitter and hard to strike out.

SECOND HITTER

The hitter next in line after the leadoff batter is also a crucial role. They have the responsibility of moving the leadoff runner into scoring position by advancing them to second or third base. On the other hand, if the leadoff hitter does not get on base, then the second batter has the duty of taking the leadoff's responsibilities. Ultimately, the characteristics that are essential to being a successful second hitter would be

1. Willingness to be a team player and doing whatever is necessary to advance the leadoff runner into scoring position.

2. Has a "good eye" and is able to wait until they get the right pitch for them to do the job that needs to be done.

3. Has good bunting skills and does not mind sacrificing their batting average for the sake of the team's offensive goals.

THIRD, FOURTH, AND FIFTH HITTER—"THE POWER PACK"

This is known as the meat of the order, signifying how important this sector of the lineup is. This group is responsible for majority of the runs that are scored for any team.

Third Hitter—The Three-Hole Hitter

The third hitter or "three-hole hitter" has been known as possibly the "best" hitter in the order. However, this is arguable because plenty of history's greatest hitters haven't always hit third in the lineup for their teams. This hitter is known for their combination of both power and ability to hit for a high batting average. Expected to have one of the highest RBI totals on the team, this player is relied on heavily in the lineup and is looked at to be consistent in their performance. They must be able to withstand the frustration of being pitched around, having pitchers avoid giving them easy pitches to hit. In other words, the three-hole hitter, given the reputation they have of usually being the best hitter on the team, will encounter opposing pitchers that are apprehensive about throwing them strikes.

Fourth Hitter—The Clean-Up

The clean-up hitter is usually the one with the most power on the team. Assuming that the previous three batters are the best on the team with getting on base, the fourth hitter is tasked with knocking everyone in. This batter usually sees majority of off-speed pitches, so while having the job of getting RBI's, they are still expected to have patience, especially given that most pitchers will attempt to pitch around them.

Fifth Hitter—The Protector

This hitter has an important job that is usually overlooked because the third and fourth hitters sometimes take all the superficial glory and hype. Their role is to protect the fourth hitter. In other words, they have to be enough of a threat that opposing teams are afraid to walk the fourth hitter because they know that the next batter could make them pay for it. A strong fifth batter will allow the three and four spot hitters to get good pitches to hit.

SIXTH-NINTH HITTERS

At younger age groups, teams are allowed to bat more than nine hitters at a time. However, for the sake of easier understanding in this discussion, we will use nine as the limit. Those who may play on a team that bats ten or eleven players, should follow the same agenda as those batting ninth. The bottom of the order sometimes holds a less desirable stigma. All good teams have a solid bottom of the order. These hitters have a great opportunity to cash in on what the meat of the order produces. They have the opportunity to deliver by piggybacking off of what the previous hitters have sparked. Once the game gets started, players who do start the game lower in the lineup may be tasked with leading an inning off once the game has gotten started.

Hitters should never take it personally when a coach puts them at a particular spot in the lineup that may be lower in the order. It's very important they do not allow friends, family, or fans to get them off their focus by telling them how they should be batting higher in the order. If a player is not careful, they will let all of this go to the head and get themselves off focus. Always remember one very important fact: **You cannot prove that you deserve to be higher in the batting order if you can't get the job done where you currently are in the lineup.**

"It's important to work on your discipline and pitch selection during practice. It will translate to the game."

Lisa Fernandez

CHAPTER 12

SWING CUSTOMIZATION: HOW TO OWN *YOUR* SWING

There is no single path one has to take to become a great hitter. Out of all the books, DVDs, seminars and camps, there are endless explanations of what a hitter should and shouldn't do. One very important factor that must be understood is that there are certain core values that are good to have for all hitters, but there will also be differences amongst all hitters. There is a sense of uniqueness.

For the swings of hitters, just like fingerprints and snowflakes, no two are the same. As a matter of fact, a hitter robs themselves of their own individuality when they attempt to follow the *exact* same path as another hitter. It's okay to borrow, observe, and learn from the swings of other players, but to attempt to *completely* mimic someone else isn't the recommended route.

Learning to personalize and customize your approach and technique is essential because it's not until you can do that that you will be able to reach your *own* natural potential. A hitter will have many coaches throughout their career if they play long enough. This means that they will receive different information from plenty of sources.

These sources can vary from those who know what's best for the hitter and those who just *think* they know what's best. Two coaches in your past or present may have given pieces of advice that oppose each other. Therefore, knowing how to decipher information and use what works for *you* is critical.

GET IN TUNE WITH YOUR SWING

To fully know yourself as a hitter, it takes a lot of self-awareness, confidence and trust in one's self. These things come with *practice*—not just any old type of practice but a detailed and focused way of practice. Since no one can feel what you feel when you take a swing, it's most ideal that *you* be the expert on your swing. It takes experimentation and experience.

It requires some alone time with your swing and an opportunity for you to go within your own thoughts and attempt to figure things out on your own. This, by no means, is implying that a private or team coach is of no use. Rather, it's something that can be done *after* a private session with a coach, for example. This way you can meditate on the ideas discussed in the private session. This forces you to think outside the box and use your *own* mental faculties to figure out what it takes to solve problems with your swing.

Experiential learning goes a lot further than listening to or watching someone else. Although, all the other methods of learning are valuable, *experiential learning*—learning through experience, learning through reflection on what has been done, and hands-on learning—can take you the furthest in your journey to becoming the best hitter you can be.

A hitter's swing can become too artificial and lack authenticity if the authenticity of the swing is not *cultivated*. It's important to use the methodology of others to arrive at your *own* conclusions. Even this book you are reading in this very moment should be used as a stepping stone to help lead you to the perfection of your *own* swing. You never want to be a "cheap version" of another hitter. A hitter can be convinced by those around them that their capabilities are not enough so much so that they start to believe they are unworthy of being great, so they figure they should simply try to be someone else.

Being taught by others can serve a purpose in helping point out the flaws that you have. Once they are pointed out, it's up to the hitter to go and try their best to perfect what new things they have learned. This is a part of being self-sufficient as a hitter. Your private or team coach will not be with you at all times, which is why you must learn to become your *own* instructor.

When you watch hitters at the college and professional level, you are looking at players who have gone through years and years of trial and error to get to where they are. They have gone through many training sessions to figure out what their strengths and weaknesses are. You're witnessing players who have gone through the ups and downs of transforming their swing in private, which affords them the ability to showcase their hard work to the world.

BRUCE LEE AND JEET KUNE DO

As mentioned earlier, Bruce Lee, the martial artist and philosopher, is widely known for his physical ability in doing karate stunts and high-flying kick moves. Yet his philosophies on mastering the skills and expertise for optimal mental focus were less celebrated. His ideas on transcending the techniques he had been taught were very controversial. The stance he took on using traditional methods as a crutch was mainly to say that he did not agree with perfecting a certain skill while blindly following the typical hand-me-down path that might have been taken in the past. He had always preached to use the information from your master teacher as a stepping stone to find your *own* truths. This can be used by hitters in the realm of batting as well.

To Bruce Lee, the traditional form of martial arts that had been so uniform and so non-individualistic was not the way he wanted to experience it. He then sought to teach his own form of martial arts, but what he planned on creating was not a one-size-fits-all type of style. After much trial and error, he came up with his own way and method of martial arts.

He called it Jeet Kune Do, which when translated means "Using no way as way." In other words, meaning not to constrain yourself to any *one* particular way of going about accomplishing goals. As long as you achieved three things, you were on the right path to finding the best way for yourself. Those three things are:

1. *Efficiency*
2. *Directness*
3. *Simplicity*

(via jeetkunedouniversity.com)

Getting rid of wasted movement is a major component of Jeet Kune Do because any style of fighting that could misuse time and energy should be done away with. This translates directly into the realm of hitting. No hitter, at any level, should take part in any form of a swing that has them using a wasted movement. For a hitter in the game of baseball or softball, it could be equivalent to having a "loop" or long swing path to the ball.

HITTING LIKE THE PROS

Customization is key and understanding *how* to customize your own separate, unique swing that is suitable for *you* is sometimes a challenge, especially because there are so many other good hitters in the world whom people would rather just copy. A very important thing for all amateur hitters to understand is that they cannot attempt to mimic every single detail of their favorite professional hitters. At little league parks around the world, kids emboldened with imagination step into the batter's box doing their best impersonation of their favorite players. This can be a double-edged sword. They can learn good things like rhythm and timing but may also pick up some habits that don't translate successfully for them.

Often, people overlook the variation between younger and older age groups in the areas of skill, physical ability, strength, coordination, and stability. For some time, there have been controversial debates about whether it's appropriate to teach younger hitters the same more complex concepts that hitters at the professional level are being taught. You can't teach a kindergartener calculus before they have learned how to add and subtract. So, it is best to keep things simpler at that younger ages. Of course, "simple" is rather subjective and could mean one thing to one individual and something completely different to another.

As athletes get older, their bodies become more sophisticated in their abilities. The increased coordination and strength allows them to have a mind-body connection that they did not have when they were younger. You may notice that when you watch professional hitters swing, they may do things that go *against* what you're taught as a youth. For example, they may dip their back shoulder and try to purposely lift the ball up and over the outfield wall.

They may have a weird, unconventional stance, funky-looking bat wiggle, and a high leg kick before the ball arrives to home plate on a pitch. Know what you *can* and cannot do when mimicking a player that is a higher level than you. This is what coaches mean when they say, "Stay within yourself." The basic core foundation for youth hitters is like training wheels on a bicycle. It allows them to stay on track with common core elements until they are ready to explore their own unique abilities.

In basketball, you would hope that a coach wouldn't teach a youth basketball player to shoot a fadeaway three-pointer like the pros of the NBA because, physically, they are less likely to be capable of doing such a thing. Many self-proclaimed hitting gurus spread information on the internet or on videos explaining to youth age kids the idea of "launch angles" and other concepts to hit the ball in the air in such a way that will help the ball travel the furthest. In theory, it may be justified at times, seeing as how all hitters would like to hit the ball as far as they can and that an objective of the game is to attempt to hit the ball with as much force as possible. However, some of these proposed ideas don't take into account *who* the hitter is or *situational hitting* that may factor in.

CHAPTER 13

THE IMPORTANCE OF A HITTER'S EYESIGHT

Eyesight is another crucial component for hitters. Without being able to see the ball optimally, it's nearly impossible to use your technique and strategy to be as effective of a hitter. The average player doesn't pay attention to their **hitter's eyesight** as it pertains to seeing the ball. Making sure that a player trains themselves to make eyesight a priority is key. How well a hitter sees the ball is a critical element. Proper technique means nothing without the ability to *see* the ball.

It goes without saying that whenever a person's head moves, their eyes move with it. Plenty of hitters have been known to have lots of movement in their pre-swing phase (or load) as well as in their contact phase of the swing. Those with high leg kicks and long strides are almost guaranteed to have lots of head movement before the swing and sometimes while making contact with the ball unless they are well-trained and cognizant of what they are doing.

A player's main objective while loading isn't just to muster up power before the swing but to manage to keep their head *still* long enough to see the ball into the hitting zone. When a batter has too much head and eye movement during the swinging process, the eyes have to make constant readjustments in order to see the incoming pitch. It's already difficult enough to be able to see a fastball, off-speed, or moving pitch heading in the batter's direction. Adding movement with the eyes and head makes it even that much harder to pick the ball up.

WAYS A HITTER CAN PRACTICE SEEING THE BALL BETTER:

1. Loading is equivalent to pulling the bowstring back on a bow and arrow. To work on keeping the head still while loading and stepping towards the pitcher, you can get creative. Make a line on the floor using tape. A player can get in their stance and start with their front foot slightly behind the line of tape and quietly step over it while practicing the loading process. Practicing stepping back and forth across the line while keeping the head and eyes still.

2. Buy an eyepatch to use for training, doing drills with an eye patch over one eye at a time.This is an unorthodox training tool, but hitters soon realize that they won't be able to see the ball without a still head. Use the patch for soft toss and front toss. It is not recommended for use in long throw batting practice.

3. Use small, different colored marks on baseballs to work on seeing the ball all the way into the zone. The objective is to have someone throw batting practice and see each ball as it crosses the plate and be able to identify what color the dots are that are painted on the ball. Usually, there are three to four dots of a particular color on the ball. You could purchase a set of balls with dots already painted on them, or you could do it yourself.

4. Work on having a quiet load. Hitters can stand in the mirror and watch themselves load while making sure they keep their heads still. They can do this by stepping with the front foot while letting the hands load simultaneously. Focus on having a soft landing on the front foot when stepping. A hard landing on the front foot will surely cause a sudden movement with the head to some extent.

5. Perform a soft toss drill where the person tossing the ball alternates tosses with

putting either a spin or no spin on the ball. Before the drill begins, agree on whether or not the hitter will swing on the "spin" or "no spin." This will help with pitch recognition.

For example, a trainer may tell a player, *"Okay, we're going to swing on the spin for this round. So, if you see a knuckling-type ball that has no spin to it, don't swing."* It's a simple and fun drill to help hitters work on pitch recognition.

In essence, when you are able to effectively keep your head *still* while batting it can feel as if the game slows down to a certain degree. Many successful hitters describe themselves as being able to *see* the ball much better during their hitting streaks. "The ball looks like a beach ball!" various hitters have proclaimed over the years when asked how they've been able to maintain a hot streak. This is because the ball appears to be moving slower. Why? The more opportunity you can give for your eyes to focus on the ball without being interrupted by head movement, the longer you give your eyes a chance to get focused on the ball as it arrives. Having a soft landing on the front foot as a hitter steps before the swing, helps them have a quieter load. (To be clear, when we refer to "quiet" in this context, it only means with less movement. It is smooth and the opposite of any "herky jerky" movement or action). A hard jab step with the front foot right before the swing could cause the head to jerk and the eyes to wobble a bit, making it hard to see the incoming ball since the eyes would have to try and refocus.

WALKS

Being able to see optimally isn't just about being able to *hit* the ball well but also being able to *not* swing at pitches that don't have good chance at being a strike. The amount of base on balls or walks is a key indicator of a mature hitter. Getting on base from watching balls isn't known as one of the coolest ways for most hitters to get on base, but it's sufficient enough to help the team, which is most important. After all, swinging at bad pitches will get you out more times than not, regardless of if you have flawless technique or not. Aside from helping the team, it helps a hitter's On Base Percentage (OBP).

Learning to take pride in taking walks in a key aspect of being the best hitter one can be. It is an indicator that a hitter doesn't chase bad pitches. From a team strategy standpoint, the more a hitter can be selective with the pitches they swing at, the greater amount of pitches the opposing pitcher will have to throw. Wearing a pitcher down is usually an advantage for the team on offense.

On the flip side, there are players who try too hard to get a walk, usually from a lack of confidence. When a hitter is not confident and prepared, they are more likely to either swing at bad pitches or not swing at all for fear that they will mess up.

It's because they may have lost confidence in their ability to perform, not because they are genuinely waiting for a good pitch to hit.

A hitter may have gone through a time period where they have been swinging at bad pitches and the embarrassment and frustration was enough to make them "gun shy" and scared to pull the trigger on the right pitches when they get them.

Getting on base through walks can sometimes help struggling hitters stay in the lineup for their team also. Frankly, if a hitter isn't doing much in the form of getting base hits, the next best option to be productive offensively is to get on base the best way they can. This, of course, would involve them *not* swinging at pitches that they don't have a good chance of being able to hit *hard*.

Swinging at good pitches in the strike zone won't *guarantee* success, but the odds will be more in the hitter's favor. The combination of luck and skill is what gives way to *chance*. It's assumed that luck is something that cannot be influenced by a player and is not something they can increase with hard work. Some would beg to differ as many high-achieving figures have been quoted attributing their luck to hard work.

"The harder I work, the luckier I get."
- Samuel Goldwyn

Though a hitter may be graced with luck from time to time, they shouldn't spend much thought on it, as they should rely on their skill and other elements that they *can* control. No serious hitter should concern their hitting agenda with luck. Letting their minds be consumed by it is only a waste of time and energy that could be spent on more productive means.

The Switch-Hitter's Eyesight

Reminder: As mentioned in Chapter 9, players new to switch-hitting deal with learning to see from a different angle. For example, right-handers who are used to seeing with their left eye as the lead eye may have to get used to seeing from the left side, where their right eye is not the lead eye. Believe it or not, aside from learning coordination from the opposite side, the next most difficult aspect is the eyesight adjustment.

"SO, I THINK THE ABILITY TO HIT —SOME GUYS HAVE IT AND SOME GUYS DON'T — BUT I THINK HOW DEDICATED YOU ARE TO TRYING TO GET THE MOST OUT OF YOURSELF, I THINK KIND OF DETERMINES HOW GOOD YOU ARE AND FOR HOW LONG. I WAS BORN WITH THE ABILITY TO HIT, BUT MY WORK ETHIC HAS TAKEN IT TO THE NEXT LEVEL."

TONY GWYNN

CHAPTER 14

THE MISCONCEPTION OF "QUICK HANDS"

You'll hear coaches talk about a hitter having "quick hands." Many times, this is interpreted the wrong way or causes players to *think* that their problems stem from them not being quick enough with swinging the bat through the hitting zone. In all honesty, having good timing and a proper swing path is a substitute for "quick hands." Some players have to compensate with a fast twitch movement, a quick swing, for the mere fact that they don't get ready before the pitch leaves the pitcher's hand, or they have a swing path that has wasted movement and is long to the ball, which can ultimately make it *look* like they are indeed slower on their swing. A player who doesn't have the correct timing or swing path will dig themselves in a deeper hole by trying to correct their swing with the "having quicker hands" approach.

When you are on time as a hitter and you have a proper and efficient swing path to the ball, there will be no need to feel that you have to rush or be "quick" with your swing.

A coach or parent making a quick hands suggestion can often make players *too* quick through the zone as they make contact with the ball. This means that their bat is only in contact with the ball for a very short period of time before it leaves the bat, meaning they have cut the swing off or, in other words, haven't extended fully. The sooner a hitter cuts off their swing, the less of a chance they have of creating backspin for the ball to carry.

You want to be quick *to* the ball, but you don't want to be quick ***through*** the ball. Quick *to* the ball involves having the most efficient swing and having the least amount of wasted movement.

Before a hitter focuses too deeply on whether they have quick hands or not they should ask themselves whether or not they are ***on time.*** So often, coaches misdiagnose a player's hitting problems as "Your hands aren't quick enough," when, in reality, it could be they they just aren't getting ready in time before the pitch is thrown. No matter how quickly your fast twitch muscles operate, if you wait until the ball is almost to the plate before you start to load and swing, then you'll be late almost every single time.. Sometimes, by luck and chance, you will happen to have your bat barrel in the zone at the right moment to connect. However, you don't want to fully rely on strictly *chance* as a hitter. Since the pitcher-hitter dual statistically is more likely to favor the pitcher in 70% of at-bats even good hitters, being ready early and on time helps the hitter be in more control in the batter's box. It helps to even the playing field.

So, when should a hitter start getting ready to swing when they are in the batter's box? Typically, a hitter should begin getting ready to hit when the pitcher starts to gather their momentum in their wind-up This should first start with the load, with the hands. Similarly to how a boxer would rear back to throw a punch is how a hitter should load in preparation to swing a bat. Essentially, the hitter and the pitcher should be winding up in unison.

There is an old saying in baseball that "When the pitcher shows you their butt, you should them yours." (This saying is obviously going to not apply for softball, since the pitcher doesn't have the same type of wind-up.) However, it basically means that as the pitcher is rearing back to deliver the pitch, you, as a hitter, should be loading your hands back getting ready to swing at the very same time. The objective is to have the front foot down and planted on the ground with the hands back and loaded, ready to swing *before* the ball arrives to the plate.

Overall, players should be spending more time focused on having the right technique and timing as opposed to compensating for lack of these two properties with trying to swing faster. Players with loopy swings, that dip their back shoulders, and who don't get their front foot down before the ball arrives into the hitting zone will *still* have issues regardless of how quick they attempt to swing the bat.

Besides having a quicker swing, some batters adjust where they stand in the batter's box. They may choose to shift towards the front of the plate or away from the pitcher in order to shorten or lengthen the distance from the pitcher's mound to the plate. Doing this could possibly be effective temporarily; however, it's only putting a band-aid on a more complicated problem.

A hitter may decide to take a step back, standing deeper in the box and closer to the opposing catcher because the pitcher is throwing fast. Doing this could make them feel like it will buy them more time to meet the ball where they wish to meet it and square it up on the barrel of the bat. However, as opposed to moving the physical location, they should be thinking about the mental adjustment that needs to be made. Instead of moving back to a deeper part of the batter's box, decide to start your loading process *sooner* and get prepared to hit earlier.

Instead of doing what needs to be done *the right way* some players will resort to just compensating for an improper way of doing things by compounding the problem with more poor habits. For example, a hitter that decides to scoot up in the box because the pitcher is throwing too slow for their liking is really just a hitter who hasn't acquired the discipline to stay back, remain balanced and wait long enough for the ball to arrive at the plate.

So instead of doing the *right* thing and waiting on the ball to get deeper into the hitting zone where contact takes place, they would rather keep the same timing approach and just change their physical proximity to the pitcher's mound. This physical adjustment could perhaps be indicative of an inability or aversion to making the mental adjustments to the hitting approach necessary.

CHAPTER 15

DOES THE TYPE OF BAT MATTER?

Many players put a major emphasis on the type or brand of bat that they use. Nothing is wrong with having a preference for a particular brand or style, but a hitter should never allow that to be the center of their focus when it comes to what is going to help them perform at their very best. Many times, a player's preference will stem from seeing *another* player have success with a certain bat.

When speaking of metal bats in amateur competition, every few years, a new brand of bat comes along with a new paint job and a unique handle grip. Per regulations, the bats are normally made of the same type of metal. For marketing purposes, they have to attempt to differentiate themselves from the competition by using fancy lingo and new names of bats to draw players in with hopes of getting new sales. It's understandable. It's just business. Nothing more, nothing less.

However, no hitter should get wrapped up in this. With the colors and textures, aluminum bats especially can be seen as somewhat of an accessory. Much like wristbands and funky colored socks, it's usually used just to make a fashion statement. There is nothing wrong with this. In fact, it can be fun. The problem is when a hitter *truly* believes that a certain bat is going to help them perform better.

A supreme hitter must never rely on any bat to make them feel complete. They know that they can get the job done with *any* bat they have in their hand. That is the mentality they *should* have.

"You can take my bat away, but you can't take my approach, attitude, focus, or technique away."

Fully and wholeheartedly accept the idea that there is no brand or type of bat that will make you the hitter that you are capable of being. You may have a preference or bat that you like based on superficial reasons that make you feel more comfortable or cool, but never believe the idea of your performance diminishing if you don't use a particular brand.

The only place where real differentiation in bats could be found is in the variation of wooden bats used in baseball. Softball doesn't use wooden bats typically, if ever. But wooden bats can range from bamboo to maple to birch to ash. Professional players that use these different types of wood could attest to a slight difference or preference for them. However, none have really been proven to differentiate to such a noticeable degree that would serve any type of advantage.

"A $200 bat won't fix a $2-dollar swing."

Bat *size* does matter, though. It matters because it factors into a hitter's capacity to exhibit bat control" which is simply the ability to direct the head of the bat, also known at the barrel or the meat of the bat, at will or with precision. At the highest levels, professional players have mismatching bat sizes. For example, you may see a bigger player use a shorter bat and a smaller player use a longer bat. The only thing that truly matters is that the hitter must be able to swing with control of the bat and have the ability to use the proper technique with it.

Preferences are fine. Things that make you as a hitter feel more comfortable in the batter's box can help put your mind at ease. Even though these things are not as important in the grand scheme, the comfort factor should never be underestimated.

Here are some small things that are more preference than of importance for hitters:

- Bat grip type
- Color of the bat
- Name brand

Bat grip is perhaps one of the biggest non-technique factors for hitters. Whether the grip is thin or thick and sticky or non-sticky are usually the different options for players.

Fact: Since we live in a right hand dominated world, most bat grips on metal bats are taped on in the direction that will be conducive to the right-handed grip. Often left-handers will experience the lumping of the handle grip because it bunches up over time due to friction.

Often, the perceived mindset that a bat offers an advantage to a hitter is only an illusion. Hitters have come up with plenty of reasons for why they imagine that a certain type of bat is better for them. They may have some friends that use it and swear that it's a bat they need. They may witness a teammate or opponent have success with a particular brand or type. Nevertheless, it's still illusionary.

How Does the Weight of the Bat Factor in?

Sometimes a player will attribute their lack of success to the weight of their bat, which could *sometimes* have an effect. However, in most cases a slight change in weight is noticeable only when the bat isn't being swung properly. In other words, a batter may have a swing with a fundamental flaw in it yet will seek to change to a lighter bat, and then get frustrated when they realize that after changing bat sizes, they still have the same issues with their technique. When dealing with troubles at the plate, a hitter must always search *within* to find what fundamental technique needs to be adjusted before changing something external like their bat or other accessories.

If you have been around the game long enough, you will have witnessed a player struggle for some time and then, out of frustration and simply not knowing what else to do, decide to rip their batting gloves off to swing with bare hands. It's not reasonable to believe that something as simple as swinging with no batting gloves would somehow change the outcome of a hitter's ability to be successful. But the superstitious nature of the sport, might make it seem as if this is something a player can do to break the cycle of bad luck.

WHY BATTERS THINK "CHOKING UP" IS NOT COOL

As opposed to being strictly **result oriented,** hitters usually allow their egos to think about the way they *look* to others. What looks cool is important to some, to such a degree that it will influence the best results they can get. For example, a hitter could be struggling with their bat control and need to choke up but won't because they do not think it looks cool. Therefore, they continue to struggle from not making the adjustment.

I find this especially prevalent among younger players. After watching their idols play on television and seeing that some of them don't choke up, it makes perfect sense why they would try to ignore instruction.

CHOKING UP VS. USING A SHORTER BAT

You have some who decide to use a shorter bat instead of choking up. They figure that you can accomplish the same agenda by just holding the bat on the knob with a shorter bat than using a longer bat and choking up on the handle. Barry Bonds famously used a shorter bat while *still* choking up on it. He had been known to mention that more barrel was always preferred since that's the aim of every hitter.

Why not just choke up and increase your chances of having the ball meet the barrel? This logic is tough to dispute even though it's a very extreme ideal to some hitters. I remember once watching Bonds give an interview and talk about his choice to choke up on the bat, and he said, "I don't like getting jammed. It hurts. If you're going to jam me, you're going to jam this!" as he pointed to the sweet spot of his barrel.

Most would believe that they cannot reach a pitch on the outside part of the plate if they choke up. Some decide to scoot closer to the plate to make up for the couple of inches of difference. If it's more practical for a hitter to choke up at the plate given the situation or circumstance of the game, they should have no problem doing it *as a team player*.

Here are the standard size recommendations based on height and weight ratio for baseball and softball:

Bat Size Chart

Your Weight (Pounds)	Your Height (Inches)									
	36-40"	41-44"	45-48"	49-52"	53-56"	57-60"	61-64"	65-68"	69-72"	73"+
Under 60	26"	27"	28"	29"	29"					
61-70	27"	27"	28"	29"	30"	30"				
71-80		28"	28"	29"	30"	30"	31"			
81-90		28"	29"	29"	30"	30"	31"	32"		
91-100		28"	29"	30"	30"	31"	31"	32"		
101-110		29"	29"	30"	30"	31"	31"	32"		
111-120		29"	29"	30"	30"	31"	31"	32"		
121-130		29"	30"	30"	30"	31"	32"	32"	32"	
131-140		29"	30"	30"	31"	31"	32"	32"	33"	
141-150			30"	30"	31"	31"	32"	33"	33"	
151-160			30"	31"	31"	32"	32"	33"	33"	33"
161-170				31"	31"	32"	32"	33"	33"	34"
171-180						32"	33"	33"	34"	34"
181 & More							33"	33"	34"	34"

Most Popular Length By Age						
Age	5 to 7	8 to 9	10	11 to 12	13 to 14	15 to 16	17 & up
Length	24-26"	26-28"	28-29"	30-31"	31-32"	32-33"	33-34"

SUPERFICIALITY IN HITTING

Those who care more about what they look like to others are also more likely to be what is called a "5:00 P.M. All-Star" (a phrase signifying the time a team may typically have batting practice for a night game). This is a player who appears to have more superficial flash or flare in comparison to how much *substance* they actually have. Substance would indicate their true ability to make an impact on offense while the superficial hitter simply looks good.

Also, known as a "Batting Practice All-Star," these types are notorious for just trying to look *pretty* during pregame warm-ups and drills instead of swinging with a true purpose in mind. These players often make everyone wonder if they would be more okay with looking pretty and getting out than simply doing what needs to be done to get the job completed for the team. There is nothing wrong with looking good. The problem comes in when a player would rather look good than help the team. If looking good costs a player the ability to help the team, it is an issue that needs to be addressed.

"THE PITCHER HAS GOT ONLY A BALL. I'VE GOT A BAT. SO, THE PERCENTAGE IN WEAPONS IS IN MY FAVOR AND I LET THE FELLOW WITH THE BALL DO THE FRETTING."

HANK AARON

CONCLUSION

LIFE LESSONS THAT
HITTING CAN TEACH US

Since we all will have to stop playing some day, it's best that we look at how our current endeavors can serve us later in life. Even society uses the act of hitting as metaphors when explaining situation.

"I asked Lisa on a date, but I *struck out*. Maybe next time."

"The teacher threw the class a *curveball* and surprised us with a pop quiz Monday morning."

So, it seems that somehow being a hitter standing in the batter's box and ready to hit a pitch has become the symbol of an individual who is navigating life's journey. In many ways, it's very fitting to say the least. In fact, many can agree that your style of hitting is indicative of the type of personality you have. Are you very aggressive at the plate and take big hacks at anything that's close? Maybe you will one day be someone who tends to jump on opportunities in the workplace or in any other societal function.

Are you patient at the plate and willing to "wait for your pitch"? This could mean that you are the type that is more laid back and wait for the opportunities to come to you. This notion doesn't indicate that everyone's hitting approach mirrors their real-life attitudes, but for many, there can certainly be a correlation.

Learning the path to the proper approach to hitting can be a precursor to acquiring the discipline that is necessary to handle challenges throughout life in general. Like hitting, life has its slumps. It has its ups and downs—it's strikeouts and home runs. It has its long stretches of periods where you might feel like nothing is going your way. Just like a slump can last for longer than it should due to lack of confidence, negative thought patterns, and refusal to analyze the situation thoroughly, life's slumps can follow the similar pattern.

The same formula that one can use to exit a slump can be the exact same approach that one can take in life when they experience a string of letdowns.

Just like in life, you can't control what the pitcher throws, you can only control how you react to the pitch. No one can get the hitter off balance, but the hitter. No one can make a hitter swing the bat, but the hitter. In life, it's not what gets thrown at you, but whether you can adjust to whatever is thrown and put a good swing on it!

Made in the USA
Middletown, DE
08 April 2022

63836110R00109